I0095126

Mixed-Race in the US and UK

CRITICAL MIXED-RACE STUDIES

Edited by Shirley Anne Tate, University of Alberta, Canada.

This series adopts a critical, interdisciplinary perspective to the study of mixed-race. It will showcase ground-breaking research in this rapidly emerging field to publish work from early career researchers as well as established scholars. The series will publish short books, monographs and edited collections on a range of topics in relation to mixed-race studies and include work from disciplines across the Humanities and Social Sciences including Sociology, History, Anthropology, Psychology, Philosophy, History, Literature, Postcolonial/Decolonial Studies and Cultural Studies.

Editorial Board: Suki Ali, LSE, UK; Ginetta Candelario, Smith College, USA; Michele Elam, Stanford University, USA; Jin Haritaworn, University of Toronto, Canada; Rebecca King O'Riain, Maynooth University, Ireland; Ann Phoenix, Institute of Education, University of London, UK; and Rhoda Reddock, University of the West Indies, Trinidad & Tobago

Previously Published:

Remi Joseph-Salisbury, *Black Mixed-Race Men: Transatlanticity, Hybridity and 'Post-Racial' Resilience* – Winner of the 2019 BSA Philip Abrams Prize

Forthcoming in this series:

Paul Ian Campbell, *Identity Politics, 'Mixed-Race' and Local Football in 21st Century Britain: Mix and Match*

Shirley Anne Tate, *Decolonizing Sambo: Transculturation, Fungibility and Black and People of Colour Futurity*

Mixed-Race in the US and UK: Comparing the Past, Present, and Future

BY

JENNIFER PATRICE SIMS

University of Alabama in Huntsville, US

and

CHINELO L. NJAKA

Peckham Rights! and Independent Social Researcher, UK

emerald
PUBLISHING

United Kingdom – North America – Japan – India – Malaysia – China

Emerald Publishing Limited
Howard House, Wagon Lane, Bingley BD16 1WA, UK

First edition 2020

Copyright © Jennifer Patrice Sims and Chinelo L. Njaka, 2020. Published under an exclusive licence.

Reprints and permissions service
Contact: permissions@emeraldinsight.com

No part of this book may be reproduced, stored in a retrieval system, transmitted in any form or by any means electronic, mechanical, photocopying, recording or otherwise without either the prior written permission of the publisher or a licence permitting restricted copying issued in the UK by The Copyright Licensing Agency and in the USA by The Copyright Clearance Center. Any opinions expressed in the chapters are those of the authors. Whilst Emerald makes every effort to ensure the quality and accuracy of its content, Emerald makes no representation implied or otherwise, as to the chapters' suitability and application and disclaims any warranties, express or implied, to their use.

British Library Cataloguing in Publication Data
A catalogue record for this book is available from the British Library

ISBN: 978-1-78769-554-2 (Print)
ISBN: 978-1-78769-553-5 (Online)
ISBN: 978-1-78769-555-9 (Epub)

INVESTOR IN PEOPLE

For Chinyere Ike, Gretha, and all the loved ones we lost along the way.

Contents

List of Tables and Figures

Chapter 2

Appendix

Acknowledgements

Thank you to Shirley Tate, Helen Beddow, Philippa Grand, Rachel Ward, Charlotte Wilson, Alice Ford, Sophie Darling, Sophie Barr, and Rajachitra. S for their work at Emerald. For reading draft chapters and providing incredibly helpful feedback we would like to thank Jeffrey Bayne, David Brunsma, Cabell Hankinson Gathman, Remi Joseph-Salisbury, Danielle Lemi, Danielle McMillian, Ijeoma Njaka, Brittany Sims, Miri Song, Christina Steidl, Myra Washington, and Paul Wright. Jenn would also like to thank her interviewees for their willingness to share their experiences; Whitney Laster Pirtle for her text message support; Erin Reid and Micah Bonds for their lightning-fast administrative assistance; and her family and friends, especially Roxie and Malcolm, for their unconditional love. Finally, Chinelo would like to thank her research participants for giving their time and sharing their perspectives; her family – husband, parents, sisters and in-laws; and friends – especially India-Alana Doris and Natoyah Epailly for their unceasing support and encouragement during the writing of this book.

Chapter 1

Introduction: The Past, Present, and Future of Mixed-Race People in the United States and United Kingdom

So, can I ask, where are you from?
Yeah, the United States.
Oh yeah? Whereabouts?
A state called Tennessee. It's in the south.
And your parents too?
My dad yes. My mom is from another southern state, South Carolina.
Hmm … were they born there?
Um, yes ….

Ten years ago, London South Bank University and London School of Economics jointly hosted a series of one-day workshops on mixed-race scholarship in the UK. The above exchange took place between a UK-based attendee and the first author, who was a US PhD student at the time. It would take another couple of trips across the pond before the underlying meaning and theoretical significance of "Where are you from?" became clear to her.

Like its US counterpart "What are you," a question with which the first author was all too familiar, the UK query "Where are you from?" is a racialised question. The workshop attendee no more wanted to know the home state of the first author's parents than people in the US wanted answers such as "a human being" when they asked "What are you?" In both cases, the question seeks a racial answer. "I'm mixed-race," "I'm Black," "I'm from Birmingham but my mum is from India and dad is from Scotland" are the types of responses askers are seeking.

Scientists know that races are not biologically predetermined subdivisions of humans but are instead socially constructed groupings.[1] Part of racialised social construction happens at the structural level in the prominence of race in laws,

---

[1]Graves 2001; López 2006; Omi and Winant 1994.

Mixed-Race in the US and UK: Comparing the Past, Present, and Future, 1–10
Copyright © 2020 by Jennifer Patrice Sims and Chinelo L. Njaka
Published under exclusive licence
doi:10.1108/978-1-78769-553-520191002

policies, and other types of legislative and political practices and thought. In other words, it is "institutional" in quality.

Another part of racial groups' social construction is at the micro-levels of interaction and symbolism. Regarding the latter, for example, race being socially constructed means that collective ideas have developed about what members of different races "look like."[2] Ideas of race-specific physical features abound: Blacks have wide noses, Whites have light skin, Native Americans have high cheek bones, and East Asians have almond-shaped eyes. How, then, does one racially classify a PhD student who has a wide nose, light skin, and almond shaped eyes?

Even when innocently intended, questions such as "What are you?" reveal the observer's racialised gaze,[3] awareness of ambiguity,[4] and sense of discomfort with a momentary crisis of racial meaning.[5] The different linguist manners and rhetorical strategies used to ask about race within the US and UK, despite both having a dominant colourblind ideology,[6] underscores how race is differentially constructed in the two nations. Their different ways of defining mixed-race on their respective censuses further reveals differential zeitgeists. And yet, whilst the available tick-boxes and the phrasing of questions greatly differ, feelings towards identity, everyday experiences, and relationships with friends and family are somewhat similar. This indicates both a broader globalisation of mixedness[7] as well as a specific transatlanticity of mixedness.[8]

The Simultaneous Emergence of Critical Mixed Race Studies in the US and UK

Over the past 30 years, social scientists and activists in the US and UK have sought to bring to light the uniquely racialised experiences of mixed-race people. Numerous contemporary mixed-race anthologies exploring identity and various lived experiences stemming from this racialised category were published in the 1990s and early 2000s.[9] From personal identity, to socialisation, to the processes by which "mixed-race" became self-enumerable on the censuses, this era of mixed-race scholarship in the US and UK has comprised and shaped the majority of English language work in the global canon. In contrast to earlier writings from the

---

[2]Kaw 1993; Maclin and Malpass 2001; Sims et al. under review.
[3]Fanon 1967; Paragg 2017.
[4]Bradshaw 1992.
[5]Omi and Winant 1994.
[6]Bonilla Silva 2018[2003].
[7]King-O'Riain et al. 2014.
[8]Joseph-Salisbury 2018.
[9]For example, Ifekwunigwe 2004; Parker and Song 2001; Perlmann and Waters 2002; Root 1992, 1996; Williams León and Nakashima 2001; Winters and DeBose 2003; Zack 1995.

nineteenth and early twentieth centuries that pathologised racialised mixture,[10] contemporary work has frequently attempted both implicitly and explicitly to construct an alternative, "positive" discourse that celebrates and empowers this "new demographic." At the same time – and seemingly in tension – some of this research has simultaneously highlighted areas of need and support "specific" for the population.[11]

Critical Mixed Race Studies (CMRS) is a relatively recent label coined to describe the global canon of interdisciplinary research focussing on racialised mixedness.[12] Formerly known as Mixed Race Studies, Daniel et al. (2014) charted the "critical turn" mixed-race scholarship has taken over the past 35 years as scholars began to incorporate race-critical theories which prioritise "race" as a subject for social inquiry around racialised disparities.[13] Though some scholars have argued that in practice the field is not very critical in their understandings and analyses of mixedness,[14] CMRS is now the institutionalised name of the field in both the US and UK.[15]

As a critical and international field, cross-cultural research has been a mainstay within CMRS. King-O'Riain et al.'s *Global Mixed Race* (2014) and Edwards et al.'s *International Perspectives on Racial and Ethnic Mixedness and Mixing* (2012), for example, both examine mixed-race populations in multiple nations.[16] There is also a rich scholarship specifically examining racial mixing and (mixed-) race construction, experiences, and identity in Brazil,[17] South Africa,[18] Canada,[19] and Puerto Rico and various Latin American countries.[20]

This book joins a nascent literature focussing on mixed-race experiences in the US and UK.[21] These two nations are often said to have a "special relationship"[22]

---

[10]Dover 1937; Gobineau 2004; Knox 1850; Stonequist 1937.

[11]Elam 2011; Ifekwunigwe 2004; Olumide 2002; Root 1992, 1996; Spencer 2010.

[12]Daniel et al. 2014.

[13]Daniel et al. 2014; Essed and Goldberg 2002.

[14]Daniel et al. 2014; Gordon 1995; Spencer 2004.

[15]For example, CMRS has been the name of academic conferences in both nations, a CMRS journal has been founded, and CMRS is the name of a new academic minor at San Francisco State University.

[16]For example, Zambia, Trinidad and Tobago, Australia, New Zealand, Mexico, Japan, Germany, Canada, etc.

[17]Daniel 2006; Hordge-Freeman 2015; Marx 1998; Nobles 2000; Osuji 2019; Telles 2006.

[18]Goldberg 1995; Laster Pirtle 2014; Marx 1998.

[19]La Flamme 2019; Mahtani 2014.

[20]Anzaldúa 1987; Loveman and Muniz 2007; Martinez-Echazabal 1998; Rodríguez 2000.

[21]Caballero 2004; Joseph-Salisbury 2018.

[22]Dumbrell (2009) observes that the idea of a US/UK "special relationship" is primarily an expectation of military, intelligence, and financial cooperation, despite politicians' proclivity for characterising it as a "partnership not just of governments but of peoples" (71). Regarding partnering governments, however, he contends that the US/UK relationship may actually be as much a result of individual politicians' (he discusses Tony Blair and George W. Bush) "personal convictions" as it is "of any

due to (common perceptions of) their shared history, language, and values; and thus they are beneficial for a study of mixedness for several reasons. Firstly, from historic mixed-race figures such as Dido Elizabeth Belle and Sally Hemmings to contemporaries such as Barack Obama, Naomi Osaka, Meghan Markle, Lewis Hamilton, Keanu Reeves, Naomi Scott, Jason Momoa, and Daniel Holtzclaw, mixed-race people have existed, prominently, in both the US and UK for centuries. Relatedly, at 2.9 per cent and 2.2 per cent of the nations' populations,[23] respectively, the percentage of mixed-race people in the US and UK is comparable.

Secondly, the nations' related but different histories offer a unique perspective on the historical rootedness of contemporary racial understandings. For instance, the importance of African enslavement in the early modern period for the development of ideas about race is shared across the Atlantic. However, the classification of people with any discernible African ancestry as Black, that is, the "one-drop" rule of hypodescent, was institutionalised in the US but not the UK, leading to differential perceptions of Black mixed-race people in the two nations. On the other hand, the two nations had different relationships with the same Asian countries. Early immigration of Indians like Bhagat Singh Thind to the mainland US versus UK overseas colonisation of the subcontinent followed by only recent immigration of Indians to the British Isles contributes to observed differences regarding contemporary racialisation of (mixed-race) Asians. In short, the outgrowth of historic similarities and differences can be seen in the current constructions of mixedness in the nations. General knowledge of these events and on-going cultural exchange also underscore how ideas about race in one nation have and continue to influence ideas about race in the other.

Theoretical Frameworks

This book uses both macro- and micro-level theoretical frameworks as well as both comparative and relational analytical frameworks. According to Omi and Winant's (1994, 2002) racial formation theory, "racial categories are created, inhabited, transformed, and destroyed" over time and space by a combination of social, historical, and political processes.[24] Racial formation theory provides a useful framework through which to investigate the particulars of racialisation processes that "locate the role of race in structuring broader social formations."[25] Omi and Winant view race as a social construct, though not one that is merely

---

structural inclination of London to follow Washington" (65). Despite acknowledging that the US and UK do share some "real world" mutual "material interests," Dumbrell argues that common beliefs about the nations' shared history, language, and values also "reflect sentiment and wishful thinking" (65). Nevertheless, in very sociological fashion, he stresses that sentiments about the special relationship "do count for something" (71).

[23]Jones and Bullock 2012; Office for National Statistics 2012a, 2012b.
[24]Omi and Winant 1994: 55, 2002: 124.
[25]HoSang and LaBennett 2012: 5.

an "ideological illusion" that influences other forms of social stratification. Race has a long, salient, and pervasive history that is significant to all social relations.[26] At the same time, race is viewed as socially and politically transient; the meanings and logistics of it are never fully fixed. It is an "unstable and 'decentered' complex of social meanings constantly being transformed by political struggle."[27] Ultimately, racial formation theory views race as a key category of social differentiation and stratification and as a shifting concept that warrants investigation and understanding.[28]

In racial formation theory, the concept of race in a given socio-historical context is understood to be constructed through both structural and cultural elements within societies. By acknowledging both of these elements in racial formation, there is room for smaller-scale – and even personal – experiences to be taken into account when examining how race functions, affects, and shapes societies alongside the larger and perhaps more widely acknowledgeable structural elements that shape racial perceptions. At this micro-level, categories like race can be understood as emerging from social interaction.[29] In other words, categories like race are "not something that people or groups *have* or are, but rather a set of actions that people *do*."[30] "Doing" race means members of society are "always involve[d in] creating groups based on perceived physical and behavioural characteristics, associating differential power and privilege with these characteristics, and then justifying the resulting inequalities."[31]

Both macro- and micro-level notions of race and racism are commonplace throughout the globe. This is due, in part, to historical meeting and clashing among people groups such as in wars, colonisation, and slave trades, as well as continuing contemporary globalisation in areas such as capitalism and media. The increasing universality of race (as a term) makes it an important and relevant focus for global and comparative sociological inquiry; however, the framing must be considered carefully. Though "race" is a common term, the specific conceptions and constructions vary across time and space. In his work on global racialisation, Dikötter (2008) notes that global racism shares "a language grounded in science ... [and] like all idioms it is rich, flexible, complex and ever evolving."[32] Thus, he argues for an interactive approach to comparisons that acknowledges the common racist beliefs that are at the root of each society's particular version of racialised meaning.

Goldberg (2009) appreciates this analytical focus on common roots but critiques Dikötter and other social scientific work on race and racism for

---

[26]HoSang and LaBennett 2012.
[27]Omi and Winant 1994: 55.
[28]Omi and Winant 2015.
[29]West and Fensermaker 1995.
[30]Markus and Moya 2010: x emphasis in original.
[31]Markus and Moya 2010: 4.
[32]Dikötter 2008: 1490.

overemphasis on "discretely conceived" sociopolitical nation states.[33] Comparisons of the US, South Africa, and Brazil, he explains, rarely focus on the shared "colonial outlooks, interests, dispositions, and arrangements [that] set the tone and terms" for race and racism in all of those nations.[34] Comparisons analogising the current situation of Palestinians in Israel to Black South Africans under apartheid, likewise in his view, too often underappreciate the role of shared history such as "apartheid South Africa's support for Israel, militarily and economically, in reciprocating Israel's willingness to consort with the apartheid state."[35]

Going beyond Dikötter's recognition of shared history, Goldberg draws on the critical work on race of "W.E.B. Du Bois, Ruth Benedict, Oliver Cromwell Cox, Frantz Fanon, Albert Memmi, Jean-Paul Sartre, Hanna Arendt, Edward Said, Stuart Hall" and others to observe that contemporary constructions of race and racism in any given location are "influenced, shaped by and fuel those elsewhere."[36] This means that "racist arrangements anywhere – in any place – depend to a smaller or larger degree on racist practice almost everywhere else."[37] Goldberg refers to race scholarship that focusses on these reciprocal interrelationships as taking a relational approach.

Though this book is subtitled "comparing" the past, present, and future, we agree with Goldberg that comparison without an analytical focus on relationality is insufficient. The analysis herein, therefore, follows in the footsteps of other CMRS work on multiple nations in that it offers both a traditional comparativist account that contrasts and compares as well as a relational account that connects. We accomplish this by identifying the similarities and differences between mixed-race in the US and UK and then discussing and explaining them in terms of both historical roots and ongoing contemporary interrelationships.

Methods and Methodology

Mixed-Race in the US and UK draws on original research projects conducted by the authors. Since some projects focussed on macro-level social phenomena and others focussed on micro-level interactions, one strength of this book is the ability to present a view of mixedness at multiple levels of society. In addition, by drawing on both sociopolitical institutions and mixed-race civil society and "regular" mixed-race people, instead of one or the other like extant literature,[38] we are able to include the perspectives of both those who have the social power to influence

---

[33]Goldberg 2009: 1272.
[34]Goldberg 2009: 1273.
[35]Goldberg 2009: 1277.
[36]Goldberg 2009: 1273–1274.
[37]Goldberg 2009: 1275.
[38]Davenport 2018: 18; see Joseph-Salisbury 2018 and Newman 2019 for recent work on mixed-race men; see Mills 2017 and Buggs 2019 for recent work on mixed-race women; see Masuoka 2017 and Hernández 2018 for recent work on political elites/socio-political institutions.

the construction of mixed-race at the structural level as well as investigate the experiences of those without institutional power who live with and/or challenge those constructions in their daily lives. In accordance with standard ethical considerations and/or at the request of some of the participants, we have anonymised the identities of all research organisations and individual participants.

Using facet methodology,[39] data for Chapters 2 and 4 were gathered by Dr Njaka through two approaches in order to examine different, complementary aspects of mixed-race construction. In the first instance, a critical discourse analysis of census reports explored the manner in which mixed-race is described and constructed in US and UK state institutions. For mixed-race civil society (comprised of groups organising around mixed-race identity and experience), in order to address both how it (re)produces mixed-race, 13 semi-structured interviews were conducted with representatives from US and UK civil society organisations (CSOs) between 2008 and 2011. Using framework analysis,[40] Dr Njaka uncovered themes that influence the descriptions and conceptions of mixed-race at each CSO.

Dr Sims' 2011–2012 interviews with 30 phenotypically racially ambiguous mixed-race adults in the US and UK are the data source for Chapters 3, 5, and 6. Admittedly, not all mixed-race individuals appear racially ambiguous, or "clearly mixed" to quote Mills[41]; and there are certainly some "mono-racial" individuals who do look racially ambiguous. Nevertheless, phenotypically racially ambiguous mixed-race adults were chosen as the study population because their racial identity is often very much an accomplished (verses rigidly ascribed) identity, meaning their experiences provide insight into the micro-performative aspects of race (i.e. "doing" race).[42] In this study, Dr Sims explored how mixed-race adults navigate ambiguity and create racial meaning in their everyday lives. Twenty-eight of the 30 interviewees identified as heterosexual, therefore the first interviews from her current project (begun in 2018) with queer mixed-race people are the data source for Chapter 7.

Outline of Chapters

Situated within a racial formation theoretical framework, Chapter 2 explores racialisation at the structural level through examining the ways that the US and UK national censuses create, shape, and maintain racialised notions within each national context. Focussing on the reporting of mixed-race, census reports are analysed qualitatively for content as well as assumptive positions in order to highlight the overall distinct ways that the US and UK use discursive practices to conceptualise mixed-race. These constructions of mixed-race then shape the ways that the rest of each nation's institutions and population understand, accept,

---

[39]Mason 2011.
[40]Ritchie and Lewis 2003.
[41]Mills 2017.
[42]Khanna and Johnson 2010; Song 2003.

and/or contest mixed-race. As becomes apparent in the analyses, the racialised categorisations at the state level are not mere descriptions of data. The aims of the census include providing a racialised narrative of the population – imbued with meanings and social consequences – and providing a framework within which individuals are allowed to categorise themselves and be recognised.

Chapter 3 on mixed-race identity examines the thought processes behind what racial category/ies mixed-race people tick on their census and other forms. Focussing on the similarities and differences in how mixed-race people in the two nations assert their identities (or not) on these forms, it reveals that though the format change to allow mixed-race race identification was welcomed by most it was not seen as a cure all to the mishaps of racial data collection or identity recording. The similar influence of the "one-drop" rule for people of African descent and the different ways nationality is combined (or not) with racial identity are also discussed.

Chapter 4 critically analyses the specific discourses generated within US and UK mixed-race CSOs. The chapter examines the ways in which CSO representatives describe and construct notions of mixed-race. The analyses highlight the variety of racialised paradigms employed by civil society that lead to a relative fluidity in racialised constructions, in contrast to their respective state entities. At times, these paradigms also include some tendencies to fall back on discourses that are reminiscent of the pathological constructions from previous centuries. The data are explored both comparatively and relationally, identifying similarities, differences, and how the states have influenced the CSOs in constructions of mixedness.

Everyday experiences within societies that hold these paradigmatic views are the topic of Chapter 5. Focussing on the different ways that mixed-race people respond to others when asked "What are you?"/"Where are you from?" the chapter explains how, to many mixed-race adults, this questioning is felt as "annoying" when posed from mono-racial people but is welcomed as an opportunity for bonding and "mixed-race solidarity" when posed from other mixed-race people. The language that mixed-race people use in response to others' "racial gaze"[43] is revealed sometimes to accommodate and sometimes to confront the expected linguistic racial norms[44] of both nations.

In addition to speaking of their own experiences and identity, Black mixed-race interviewees also discussed how racial considerations influenced their dating and plans for having children; and those who were already partnered with children discussed how race intersected with parenting. Chapter 6 thus focusses on the family planning and parenting experiences of mixed-race adults. Juxtaposing Sims' US interviewees with the accounts of the UK parents in Song's (2017) *Multiracial Parents: Mixed Families, Generational Change, and the Future of Race*, the chapter reveals the similarities and differences in mixed-race adults' families "a generation down" in the two nations.

---

[43]Fanon 1967; Paragg 2017.
[44]Cazenave 2015.

In response to the heteronormativity of Chapter 6 and the broader CMRS literature in general, Chapter 7 highlights the limited extant research on queer mixed-race populations. It then presents preliminary findings from Sims' current interview study of queer mixed-race people apropos to current theories about the influence of peer relationships and interactions on the identity development of Black mixed-race men and women. The early emerging patterns underscore how race and sexuality are mutually constituting systems of oppression.[45]

The final substantive chapter briefly summarises the major themes of the book. The chapter then turns a forward eye to consider future events that may influence mixed-race people in the US and UK as well as emerging avenues of research in CMRS. The book concludes with a Methodological Appendix. The first part provides an in-depth accounting of each author's research methods. Following this and drawing on the experiences of both authors, it then offers a discussion of some of the processes, challenges, and benefits of conducting qualitative research in two nations. The chapter – and book – ends by looking beyond the US and UK specifically to consider issues in conducting multinational qualitative research in general.

The multifaceted and interrelated ways that mixed-race is socially constructed links the chapters together. Whether focussing on the macro-level or the micro-level, or whether comparing or showing relationality, we demonstrate that mixed-race both challenges and exists alongside traditional White supremacist notions of race.

Notes on Terminology

Sociolinguists within CMRS have observed that "[f]rom the mid-20th century on, we have seen a dramatic increase in broader, more open-ended terms that reflect a society that sees more racial categories."[46] In addition to biracial, multiracial, and mixed-race, new terms such as Hapa, Hafu, and "a dizzying array of other portmanteau words for every possible ethnic combination" such as "Blasian" have joined the English lexicon.[47] In this book, we use the term "mixed-race" to describe populations in either nation that identify as "more than one race" or "two or more races" (US) and as a "mixed ethnicity" or "mixed ethnic" (UK). We also used mixed-race to indicate people whose immediate parentage consists of members from two or more socially constructed racial groups, though when they do not personally identify as "mixed-race" their racial identity is included as well (e.g. mixed-race Filipino and Black-identified mixed-race).

The term "mixed-race" tends to be the most frequently used and understood term among the different populations and organisations in both national contexts. Moreover, this term allows us to analyse data from two nations that use different terminologies without bias towards one or other government's choice

---

[45]Crenshaw 1989; Vidal-Ortiz et al. 2018.
[46]Holiday 2019.
[47]Holiday 2019; Washington 2017.

for official terminology. When we are writing about a specific national context, however, we use the official terminology from the respective census form inter-changeably with "mixed-race."

We use several acronyms throughout the book. As noted above, CMRS stands for the interdisciplinary academic field of Critical Mixed Race Studies. We use US (or US American) to refer to the nation and people of the United States of America; and we use UK to refer to the United Kingdom of Great Britain and Northern Ireland. Although a large portion of our UK research was conducted from England, our data reflects the entire nation, unless otherwise noted (e.g. when referring to the census). The US Office of Management and Budget is abbreviated as OMB; and the UK Office for National Statistics is ONS. CSO refers to civil society organisation. LGBTQIA stands for Lesbian, Gay, Bisexual, Transgender, Queer, Intersex, and Asexual, and is used to denote the diverse community composed of individuals who identify thusly.

Chapter 2

Creating Mixed-Race: The Census in the US and the UK

The US and the UK are among the majority of countries in the world that conduct regular national censuses.[1] The complex exercise of the census aims to provide a complete survey of a national population. Not only does this include the number of inhabitants, but also various other demographic information relating to age, gender, race/ethnicity, national origin, religion, and other social and economic data. As the United Nations frames it, ultimately the national census is about assessing and understanding human capital – the most important capital in contemporary society. Thus, the national census provides data that are the *sine qua non* for quantifying and qualifying the human capital within a nation's borders.[2]

Theoretically, the national census exercise is an unbiased assessment of a population, however practically, this is not the case. Both the US and the UK conduct decennial censuses that are organised by the state. The US Census Bureau (within the Office of Management and Budget, OMB) and the Office for National Statistics (ONS) in the UK oversee the enumeration of the entire national population, data analysis, and information dissemination to various organisations and members of the public. The census process is thus an authoritative and representative[3] exercise that is embedded with the power dynamics of the state.

Only a certain number of groups are constructed as meaningful and distinct in a given society, thereby contributing to, encouraging, and maintaining social stratification. Responses outside of the provided group options are either recategorised to recognised groups or omitted entirely, further reifying the provided racialised options.[4]

---

[1]United Nations 2017.
[2]United Nations 2017.
[3]The accuracy of representation is limited by the documented disproportional undercounting of racialised minorities in both nations (see Choldin 1994; Prewitt 2000; Simpson 2003; Teague 2000).
[4]Anderson 1991; Kertzer and Arel 2002; Perlmann and Waters 2002.

Mixed-Race in the US and UK: Comparing the Past, Present, and Future, 11–27
Copyright © 2020 by Jennifer Patrice Sims and Chinelo L. Njaka
Published under exclusive licence
doi:10.1108/978-1-78769-553-520191003

The questions and categories are decided upon by state officials and then the categories are "officialised" through their subsequent adoption as default classification options for other state institutions (e.g. education, family services, and health organisations) as well as civil society bodies (voluntary and community organisations and other entities independent of the government). In this way, these state-made categories thus limit the ways individuals see and can categorise themselves officially.[5] Consequently, the state has a significant role in setting the parameters for its people vis-à-vis personal and collective identity.

This chapter examines race on the US and UK[6] censuses. After a brief historical overview, it explores each nation's discourses around "race" and "ethnicity." It examines the specific set of terminology used by each census organisation to classify people with more than one racialised identity, thereby revealing differing conceptualisations of mixed-race. The chapter also provides descriptive statistics on the mixed-race populations in both nations. The US OMB and the UK ONS reports and related policy documents, published based on census data, reveal how the governments' presentation and interpretation of data influence the social construction of mixed-race people. Concurrently, the ways that mixed-race individuals have engaged with the categories reveals how state constructions remain susceptible to differential individual interpretation.

Race on the Census: A Brief History

Within racial formation theory, the macro-level racial project plays a central role. Michael Omi and Howard Winant (1994, 2015) conceptualise the state as setting racialised agenda and positions, to which micro-level racial projects then either comply or resist. This process creates and refines racialised constructions within a given context. The national census is one such macro-level project that has long played an important role in ascribing racialised identity onto individuals through categorisation.

Race in the US is associated strongly with classification and categorisation status.[7] Thus, it is not surprising that the US has always had race embedded in its census. There has been a race question on every US census since the first enumeration in 1790. Historically, racialised status was a criterion for the right to be counted as a free and full human being, and further reveals the significance

---

[5]Anderson 1991; Kertzer and Arel 2002.

[6]The United Kingdom of Great Britain and Northern Ireland enumerates the population using separate, different census forms for England and Wales, Scotland, and Northern Ireland. The way that each form asks about ethnicity varies (i.e. question format and ethnicity options). Subsequently, the amalgamated UK data is only partially comparable. For this reason, the UK census analyses focus on the England and Wales data, however most of the findings are generally applicable for the whole of the UK.

[7]Olumide 2002.

of the racialised designations of "White" and "Black" within this national context.[8,9] In contrast, although the UK has conducted censuses since 1801, an explicit "ethnicity" question to categorise by racialised group was not included until 1991, though questions of ancestry and place of birth functioned to assess racialised identity in previous census cycles.

Each nation's census body has a distinct approach to constructing and conceptualising race through its practices and discourse. In this manner, these constructions and conceptualisations fit into the larger racialised categorisation processes of each nation. The terminologies that each state uses to categorise racialised difference reveal much about the larger racialised ideology imbued within each society. The US Census Bureau uses the term "race" for six discrete overall categories: "White," "Black or African American," "American Indian and Alaska Native," "Asian," "Native Hawaiian and Other Pacific Islander," and "Some other race." The classifications for these groups are based on a combination of racialised colour labels (i.e. White and Black), continental origin (i.e. Asian), and/or US state/national/regional origin (e.g. Alaska Native, Samoan, and American Indian). This is in addition to the government's notion of "ethnicity." On the US census, ethnicity refers only to Hispanophone origins in Latin America or the country of Spain.[10] Specifically, the OMB defines "Hispanic or Latino"[11] ethnicity as "a person of Cuban, Mexican, Puerto Rican, South or Central American, or other Spanish culture or origin,[12] regardless of race."[13] Therefore, the two official ethnicities recognised are "Hispanic or Latino" and "Not Hispanic or Latino."[14] Ethnicity is said to be "distinct" from race; there is a separate question for it on

---

[8]Gibson and Jung 2002.

[9]Only people racialised as White were counted as full human beings in the early US censuses. Not only was that group the only one afforded rights as US citizens, but also to be afforded mere acknowledgement as human beings and as full members of the US population. In accordance to the Three-Fifths Compromise of 1787, some Native Americans were not counted on the census and Black slaves were counted as only three-fifths of a person (Alexander 2012).

[10]Hochschild et al. 2012; Jones and Smith 2001: 7.

[11]The term "Hispanic or Latino" directly reflects the wording of the US Census Bureau and the OMB. Their language has not been updated to reflect the current shifts that use gender-inclusive terminologies (i.e. Latinx) and move away from the term, "Hispanic."

[12]As outlined in the OMB directive paper (1997) and the census analyses, the term "origin" is used as a distinguisher of the different racial and ethnic categories. As both refer to "origin," there is no obvious difference as to why Asian or African origins distinguish people groups by "race" whilst Spanish and Central and South American (except for Brazilian Lusophone) origin require the additional identifier of "ethnicity." This is further curious, as Central and South Americans are also examples given for the "American Indian and Alaska Native" race category and those with ancestry from Spain (as part of Europe) are given as part of the "White" race category.

[13]Jones and Smith 2001: 7.

[14]OMB 1997: 11.

the census, and one who responds with Hispanic or Latino ethnicity may also select any racialised category or categories to answer the race question (Fig 2.1).[15]

Other race options that could otherwise be constructed in comparable "ethnic terms" (e.g. Asian or Pacific Islander groups currently enumerated as "race" or Arab or African groups, which are not specifically asked about on the census, but could be constructed similarly to Hispanicity around language, colonial histories, and/or other geopolitical histories) do not have the same logic applied to them. Furthermore, "ethnicity" is not exclusively used to refer to Spanish or Latin American origin in popular usage. For example, "ethnicity" is commonly used to establish personal identity and connection to familial immigration histories, particularly for those who can be racialised as White.[16] Therefore, identifiers such as Scottish American, Irish American, Italian American, and Jewish American are commonly understood to be references to ethnicity in a way distinct from the US census. In this popular sense, what can be termed "symbolic" or "optional" ethnicity[17] is *generally* not as susceptible to comparable levels of systemic discrimination as racialised ethnicities and subsequently is not monitored via census data. Regardless, what becomes clear is the discourse around official "ethnicity" and its "separate distinction" from "race" is ambiguous in its articulation and practice at best and illogical at worst.

Moreover, the US is unique among most nations in its enumeration of "race" and "ethnicity" separately. Instead, research has found that most nations use *either* "race" *or* "ethnicity" to enumerate group-based identity. Additionally, the US is alone in specifically targeting a specific ethnic group for an ethnicity question.[18] The distinction of the two concepts for official purposes is a uniquely US discursive construction; specifically, that the only official ethnic option for the US population is the concept of Hispanicity.

The development of and reason for "race" and "ethnicity" as distinct and separate concepts is not well articulated in the census analysis publications. According to the OMB directive standards that guide census categories, both "race" and "ethnicity" categories are not intended to imply biological or genetic references and are suggested to include social and cultural characteristics, in addition to ancestry.[19] To the extent of meaning and distinction, the only additional stipulation regarding the use of these terms is that they reflect "clear and generally understood definitions that can achieve broad public acceptance."[20]

In the UK, the ONS refrains from using the term "race" on the census. This is reflective of increased political unease with racial terminologies in Great Britain and Northern Ireland during the 1970s and 1980s. During this time, prevailing political thought suggested that to use "race" would cause offense to both

---

[15]Humes et al. 2011: 2; Jones and Smith 2001: 7; OMB 1997.
[16]Song 2003; Waters 1990.
[17]Gans 1979; Morning 2008; Waters 1990.
[18]Morning 2008.
[19]OMB 1997.
[20]OMB 1997: 2.

Reproduction of the US Census Questions on Ethnicity and Race

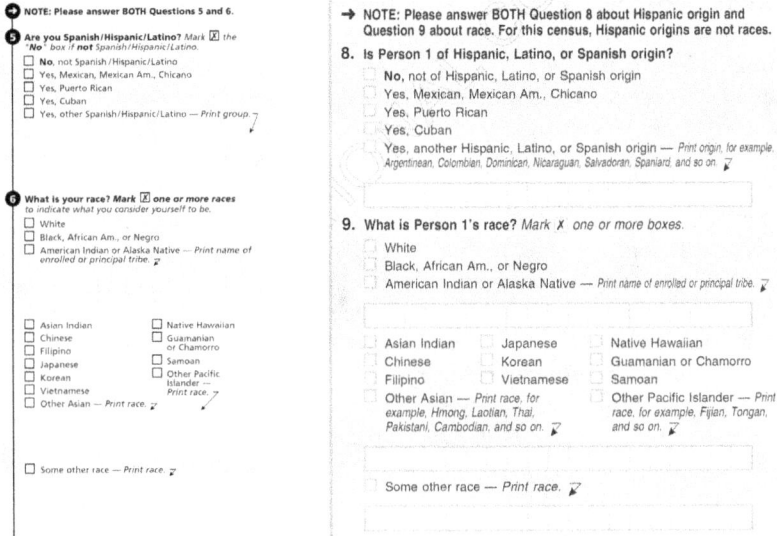

Source: US Census Bureau, Office of Management and Budget
2000 Census Questionnaire

Source: US Census Bureau, Office of Management and Budget
2010 Census Questionnaire

Fig. 2.1.   Reproduction of the US Census Questions on Ethnicity and Race.

non-White and White census respondents. Furthermore, politicians viewed it impossible to define "race" or "colour" in precise enough terms to yield meaningful results.[21] This fits into a larger national stance of using "multiculturalism" to justify not counting its population by race.[22] Under this premise, the UK likened itself to be a nation welcoming of immigrants, and thus racial and cultural mixing were positioned as offering a politically and ideologically positive value to UK society.[23] According to Debra Thompson, "The thrust of this approach lies in the tendency to valorise [*sic.*] racial mixing by not counting race, which emphasises racial hybridity beyond the necessity of counting."[24] However, with the increasing pressure to improve enforcement of the Race Relations Act passed in 1968 and a wider acknowledgement for the need of racialised data to monitor civil rights more broadly, the UK introduced an "ethnicity" question to the 1991 census.

As the ONS views the ethnic categories as self-defined, directive documents do not outline specifically what the available ethnic categories mean, either to those bodies collecting and using the data or for whom the specified categories are intended. However, there are detailed recoding documents that ONS statisticians

---

[21]Kertzer and Arel 2002; Thompson 2015.

[22]Thompson 2015.

[23]Rallu et al. 2004; Thompson 2015.

[24]Thompson 2015: 122.

use to "correct" ethnic selections, in cases where more than one ethnicity is selected, where there is an assumed incongruence between marked and written-in responses, or other responses deemed as "nonsense."[25] Intrinsically, this reveals a contradiction, as there are instances where responses can be altered from the way respondents originally identify themselves and family members. The ONS does indeed operate with a rigid construction of racialisation that influences which responses are flagged for recoding. If one falls outside of the categories offered, they are relegated to alternative categories accepted by the state.

Smaller populations often are relegated to "Other" ethnicities. Consequently, these populations are potentially obscured in the census data as they are likely to describe their ethnic affinities in multiple ways. They are not as easily categorised as the larger populations with official categories, and thus smaller populations remain unrepresented. This greatly impacts the ways that race is constructed, both officially and throughout society.

Though the UK question uses the term "ethnicity," one of the purposes of the data is to "monitor possible *racial* disadvantage within minority groups,"[26] which suggests synonymy between understood notions of "race" and "ethnicity" at a discursive level. "Ethnicity" classifies groups based on a combination of racialised colour labels (i.e. White and Black), continental origin (i.e. African and Asian), and/or national/regional origin (e.g. Irish, Caribbean and Chinese). In England and Wales, the 2001 census form offered the following ethnic options: "White," "Mixed," "Asian or Asian British," "Black or Black British," and "Chinese or other ethnic group."[27] These five main categories are listed, followed by further specified subgroups for each ethnic option. There is some variation to the level of differentiation within these subgroups: country (e.g. "Irish"), multicountry/regional (e.g. "British" or "Caribbean"), and continental (e.g. "African"). "Colour" (phenotype) is not used as a sole marker of ethnic differentiation on any UK censuses, as it is not possible to select only "White" or "Black." Where colour is used as an overall category on the census, there are subcategories to qualify the ethnic descriptor, which is distinct from the US census, which does not always do so. Although official census forms in the UK do not use sole colour referents to ethnicity, they are at times used as ethnic labels in the analysis reports.[28]

Within the White, Asian, and Chinese categories, limited subcategories offer national origin identification for further specification. Additionally, there is an option for write-in responses to "Any other" ethnic background. For the Black category, the subcategory options are also present, but less specific: "Caribbean" and "African." Superficially, "Caribbean" refers to a region of 26 countries (half within the UK Commonwealth), whilst "African" is a demonym for the continent of Africa, which is made up of 54 nations (Fig. 2.2).

---

[25]ONS 2003, 2015; White Paper 2003.
[26]White Paper 1999: 15, emphasis added.
[27]Bradford 2006: 8.
[28]For example, Bradford 2006.

Reproduction of the UK Census Questions on Ethnicity

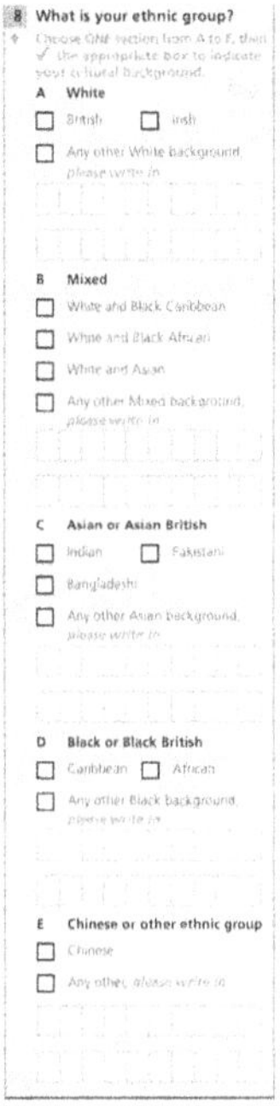

8 What is your ethnic group?
Choose ONE section from A to E, then ✓ the appropriate box to indicate your cultural background.
A White
British
Irish
Any other White background, please write in
B Mixed
White and Black Caribbean
White and Black African
White and Asian
Any other Mixed background, please write in
C Asian or Asian British
Indian
Pakistani
Bangladeshi
Any other Asian background, please write in
D Black or Black British
Caribbean
African
Any other Black background, please write in
E Chinese or other ethnic group
Chinese
Any other, please write in

Source: Office for National Statistics
Licensed under the Open Government Licence v.3.0
2001 Census Questionnaire, England

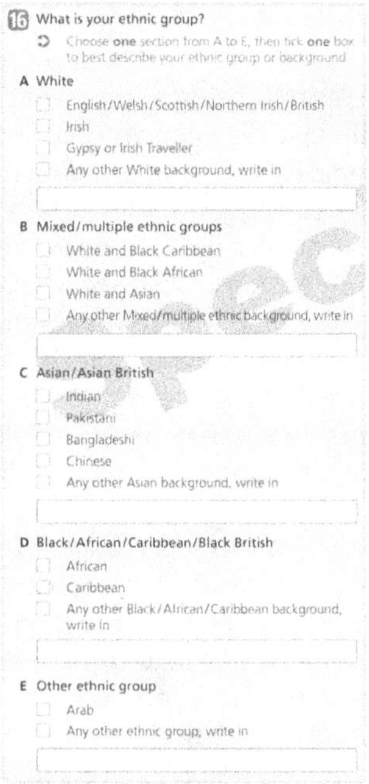

16 What is your ethnic group?
Choose **one** section from A to E, then tick **one** box to best describe your ethnic group or background
A White
English/Welsh/Scottish/Northern Irish/British
Irish
Gypsy or Irish Traveller
Any other White background, write in
B Mixed/multiple ethnic groups
White and Black Caribbean
White and Black African
White and Asian
Any other Mixed/multiple ethnic background, write in
C Asian/Asian British
Indian
Pakistani
Bangladeshi
Chinese
Any other Asian background, write in
D Black/African/Caribbean/Black British
African
Caribbean
Any other Black/African/Caribbean background, write in
E Other ethnic group
Arab
Any other ethnic group, write in

Source: Office for National Statistics
Licensed under the Open Government Licence v.3.0
2011 Census Questionnaire, England

Fig. 2.2. Reproduction of the UK Census Questions on Ethnicity.

The Addition of Mixed-Race Identification

Since the late twentieth century, an increasing number of individuals in both nations are choosing to identify as more than one racialised category. A significant number of respondents during the 1990 (US) and 1991 (UK) census cycles indicated racialised mixedness outside of the provided, discretely racialised categories. In response to this and, in the US, a sustained grassroots campaign; both the US and UK added response options for the 2000 (US) and 2001 (UK) census cycles to allow individuals to identify themselves as being more than one race. Whilst this was the first time mixed-race identity was enumerated in UK census history, the US has previously enumerated for specific constructions of mixedness in its history. From 1850 to 1870, 1890, 1910, and 1920[29]; census enumerators were instructed to identify "Mulattos" or persons of White and Black racialised heritage. In 1890, enumerators further had to identify "Quadroons" (persons

[29]Although it was illegal during this point in US history, there still was Black/White sexual union, and an extensive "Mulatto" population was reported during these censuses (Perlmann and Waters 2002).

with a quarter of Black ancestry) and "Octoroons" (persons with an eighth of Black ancestry) as subcategories of "Mulatto." However, 2000 was the first time that mixed-race could be indicated since self-enumeration began in 1970, and the first time that racialised mixture could be captured outside of an exclusive Black/White binary.

Although the changes (and the accompanying lead up) occurred around the same time in both nations at the turn of the twenty-first century, each state nonetheless developed a different set of terminologies to refer to this population of respondents. In the US, mixed-race individuals were given the opportunity to mark one or more racialised category. The UK census created a new "Mixed Ethnicity" category, with four subcategory options from which to select: "White and Black African," "White and Black Caribbean," and "White and Asian"; which vary in national/continental specificity. As with the other ethnic group options, there is also a fourth option, "Any other Mixed background," which is available for write-in responses.[30] For the 2011 census, the "Mixed" category was changed to read: "Mixed/Multiple Ethnic Groups."[31]

The US census has refrained from adding a mixed-race category with selected subcategories to its race question, as was done in the UK. Instead, in 2000 the Census Bureau allowed for respondents to select more than one racialised category for the first time in its census history. Those who were coded into more than one racial category were referred to in analyses as the "Two or More races" population, or as those who identified as "More than one race."[32] In effect, by disallowing a "catch all" category (or categories, as in the case of the UK), the OMB avoided creating another official racialised category alongside the existing ones. The socio-historical landscape in the US is such that creating additional racial categories is wrought with political implication for the existing racial order. Leading up to the change in the race question in 2000, broader civil rights organisations resisted the addition of a mixed-race category to the census. The primary reason for this was concern of diverting race selection away from the existing categories, thus lowering the overall counts and diminishing the ability to monitor and enforce civil rights for the existing racialised groups.[33] The OMB's decision to

---

[30]Bradford 2006: 8.

[31]The England and Wales 2011 census cycle introduced changes to the wording of the broad ethnic categories, though the changes were deemed minor enough by the ONS to render the 2001 and 2011 data as "broadly comparable" (ONS 2012a). The "Mixed" ethnicity category was altered to "Mixed/Multiple Ethnic Groups." The subcategories retained the same wording from the 2001 census cycle. "Asian or Asian British" changed to "Asian/Asian British" and "Chinese" was consolidated under the Asian category. "Black/African/Caribbean/Black British" replaced "Black or Black British," with no changes to the subcategories. The "Other" ethnic group added the subcategory "Arab" alongside "Any other ethnic group." The ONS plans to continue using this revised wording for the 2021 census cycle (HM Government 2018, ONS 2012b).

[32]Jones and Smith 2001: 1, 2.

[33]Williams 2005.

allow respondents to "mark one or more" race assuaged these concerns. Furthermore, by subsequently tabulating and analysing the data alongside "race alone" responses, the numbers for each race increased when respondents had the more flexible option to selection multiple responses.[34]

Counting Mixed-Race: The Numbers

Turning to the actual counts recorded for the race question in each country is an important way to further contextualise the mixed-race populations in each nation. Indeed, the mere counting by race implies that there is something to count in the first place.[35] Exploring the breakdown of numbers and percentages provides an opportunity to compare the mixed-race populations of each nation, and highlights which details each nation deems salient. The numbers represent the pivotal space where the categories developed by state institutions are operationalised through the responses of the general public.

In 2001, the total population for England and Wales was 52,359,976. Of this, 1.3 per cent selected from the Mixed ethnicity category.[36] In 2011, the general population rose 7.1 per cent to 56,075,912. Mixed/Multiple ethnicity rose to 2.2 per cent of the population, increasing 82.2 per cent in number.[37] Looking at subcategories, the Mixed White and Black Caribbean subcategory made up 0.5 per cent of the Mixed group population in 2001, rising to 0.8 per cent in 2011. The proportion of Mixed White and Black African responses was 0.2 per cent in 2001 and 0.3 per cent in 2011. The Mixed White and Asian subcategory was 0.4 per cent in 2001, rising to 0.6 per cent in 2011. The Mixed Other group represented 0.3 per cent of the Mixed category in 2001, increasing to 0.5 per cent in 2011.[38]

According to the US Census 2000, the population in the US totalled 281,421,906,[39] and the Two or More races population made up 2.4 per cent of the total population.[40] The 2010 US census reported the total population as 308,745,538, which represents a 9.7 per cent increase from census 2000.[41] Of this, 97.1 per cent of the population selected One race (9.2 per cent increase in number from 2000) and 2.9 per cent selected Two or More races (32.0 per cent population increase from 2000).

Of the 2001 mixed-race population, the percentage of respondents that selected Two races was 93.3 per cent. The largest groups within the Two races subcategory were White and Some Other Race (32.3 per cent of the Two or More

[34]Williams 2005.
[35]Nobles 2000, 2002.
[36]Berthoud 1998; Jivraj 2012; Rendall 2005.
[37]Jivraj 2012; White 2012.
[38]Jivraj 2012; Rendall 2005; White 2012.
[39]Grieco and Cassidy 2001, Njaka 2013a.
[40]Grieco and Cassidy 2001; Humes et al. 2011; Njaka 2013a.
[41]Jones and Bullock 2012; Njaka 2013a.

races category), White and American Indian or Alaska Native (15.9 per cent), White and Asian (12.7 per cent), White and Black or African American (11.5 per cent), and Black or African American and Some Other Race (6.1 per cent). The remaining Two races responses each represented under 4.0 per cent. The proportion of Three races responses was 6.0 per cent of the Two or More races group, with only two of these subcategories reaching over 1.0 per cent of the total Two or More races population: White, Black or African American, and American Indian and Alaska Native (1.6 per cent), and White, Asian, and Native Hawaiian and Other Pacific Islander (1.3 per cent). The Four races subcategory made up 0.6 per cent of the Two or More races category. The White, Black or African American, American Indian and Alaska Native, and Asian response represented 0.2 per cent of the Two or More races population; the remaining combinations totalled 0.1 per cent or less. The Five races category represented 0.1 per cent of the multiple responses, with a majority selecting White, Black or African American, American Indian and Alaska Native, Asian, and Native Hawaiian and Other Pacific Islander (0.1 per cent). Respondents who selected all six racialised categories reached a percentage that rounded to 0.0 per cent (823 respondents or 0.0003 per cent of the total population).[42]

Over nine million US respondents selected more than one race in 2010 (9,009,073 responses).[43] Those selecting Two races represented 91.7 per cent of the Two or More races population, reflecting a +29.8 per cent change in number from 2000 to 2010. White and Black or African American was the largest group reported, making up 20.4 per cent of the Two or More races population and a 133.7 per cent increase from the 2000 census. White and Some Other Race (19.3 per cent, −21.1 per cent change), White and Asian (18.0 per cent, +86.9 per cent change), White and American Indian and Alaska Native (15.9 per cent, +32.3 per cent change), and Black or African American and Some Other Race (3.5 per cent, −24.6 per cent change) reflect the most common combinations selected by respondents. The Three races category represented 7.5 per cent of the Two or More group, which reflects a 64.9 per cent increase from 2000. As seen in 2000, only two subcategories reached over 1.0 per cent in 2010: White, Black or African American, and American Indian and Alaska Native (2.6 per cent, +105.7 per cent change from 2000), and White, Asian, and Native Hawaiian and Pacific Islander (1.6 per cent, +59.7 per cent change). Respondents selecting Four races represented 0.6 per cent of the Two or More population, which indicates a 50.7 per cent increase from the previous census. The largest combination within this group was again the White, Black, or African American, American Indian and Alaska Native, and Asian subcategory (0.2 per cent, +78.2 per cent change from 2000). The remaining combinations remained under 0.1 per cent, as in Census 2000. The Five races subcategory comprised 0.1 per cent of the Two or More population, with a count that reflected a 0.2 per cent decrease from 2000. White, Black or African American, American Indian and Alaska Native, Asian,

---

[42]Grieco and Cassidy 2001; Humes et al. 2011.
[43]Humes et al. 2011; Jones and Bullock 2012; Pew Research Center 2015.

and Native Hawaiian and Pacific Islander was the largest combination within this subcategory and represented 0.1 per cent (−0.1 per cent change from 2000). The other percentages of possible combinations for Five races rounded to 0.0 per cent. The same is the case for the Six race subcategory, which was recorded as 0.0 per cent (792 respondents). That population count represents a decrease of 3.8 per cent from 2000.[44]

Government Reporting on Mixed-Race Data

The racialised ideologies in each nation not only influenced the terminologies selected, but further guided the subsequent analyses of these populations and the data comparisons with other racialised groups. Following each decennial census, the OMB and the ONS publish a series of publications detailing their findings. The set of reports focusses on both general demographic information and what the OMB or ONS deem particularly salient for the specific census cycle. The census reports become the sites of official racialised discourse from the state. Arguably, one of the most significant ways that the US and the UK use the census is for determining and reinforcing racialised categories.

The differences in the varying interpretations of mixed-race are important when considering how the data for people racialised as mixed were analysed in both countries. US "ethnicity" (i.e. "Hispanic or Latino") aside, more than one race was regarded as a multiplicity of identities in the US, comprising as many races as a respondent selected.[45] The language used to discuss this population was consistent with this; the group were not spoken about as one homogeneous group, but rather as the population that responded as being more than one race. For example, in analyses, the racial data were "divided into two broad categories: the race *alone* population and the *Two or more races* population."[46] The data are reported both in the broad category of "Two or More races," as well as in subcategories specifying the number of races selected (i.e. "Two races," up to "Six races"). However, as there were relatively few respondents who chose more than two races in the Two or More group (approximately 7.0 per cent of the Two or More population), the group is frequently discussed in terms of the two broad categories mentioned above.

For the UK analyses, those respondents who indicated more than one ethnicity were frequently categorised into one "Mixed" group. "Mixed" was often described as a single identity, opposed to multiple or fluid racialised identities that can potentially include more than the options offered. Examples in language include, "… people who have *a* Mixed ethnic identity" and "This article profiles the *four* Mixed ethnic groups identified in the 2001 Census."[47] Throughout the census reports that focussed on Mixed ethnicity, the four specific Mixed groups

---

[44]Humes et al. 2011; Jones and Bullock 2012.
[45]Jones and Bullock 2012; Jones and Smith 2001.
[46]Jones and Bullock 2012: 3; Jones and Smith 2001: 2, emphases in original.
[47]Bradford 2006: 3, emphases added.

(including "Other Mixed") are spoken about mostly as separate and distinct groups, and their reported characteristics are presented as such. In the more general articles on the mixed-race population in the census results, "Mixed ethnic" was used more frequently in the general sense, as well as the term "Mixed race." The introduction of "Mixed race" goes undefined by the government reports; however, it is used as an apparent synonym to "Mixed ethnicity." An example of this usage is from the Victims of Crime summary in the "Focus on Ethnicity and Identity" article, where the term "Mixed race" is used numerous times to refer to "people," "background(s)," and "households"; including an instance in the topic subtitle.[48] The term "Mixed ethnic(ity)" is not used in this section of the article, however when "Mixed race" is compared to other groups, the other groups are specified to be "ethnic" – and not "racial" – groups. This suggests that the ONS conceptualises "ethnicity" as racialised terminology, rather than distinguishing between the two concepts in a meaningful way.

Another difference is the way that the UK and the US describe mixed-race populations regarding racialised majority/minority status. In the UK reports, the Mixed ethnic groups are labelled and constructed as "new ethnic minorities" that have only recently emerged since the 1950s.[49] However, racialised mixedness has been occurring for centuries in both the UK and the US. In summary reports, "Mixed ethnicity" is regarded as non-White, and is therefore considered to be a minority ethnic population in the UK.[50] An example of such wording can be found in the "Focus on Ethnicity and Identity" article, where it is written, "Fifteen per cent of the non-White population were from the Mixed ethnic group."[51] Latent in this statement is the negating of the White ethnicities in the majority of the Mixed ethnic groups, as the three main groups as defined by the ONS all include White (e.g. "White and Black Caribbean"). For the purposes of the UK government, indicating a racialised minority identity alongside a White one classifies Mixed ethnic respondents as ethnically minoritised, which suggests a form of binary and hypodescendent understanding of racialisation. It is unclear whether any exceptions are made in the cases of the write-in responses for the Other Mixed groups, where respondents indicated two White ethnicities (e.g. White British and White Irish). For the White Irish generally, even though they are considered an ethnic minority by the ONS, they are also classified as White in the "Focus on Ethnicity and Identity" report,[52] and thus aggregated into the White ethnic majority. The Other Mixed group is not spoken about in depth in this report, where the main racialised groups are compared.

A different approach is taken by the US Census Bureau in the way it describes the respondents of the Two or More racial category. The reports for the US do not use majority or minority terminology to qualify their racialised categories,

---

[48]Rendall 2005: 14.
[49]Bradford 2006.
[50]Bradford 2006; Rendall 2005.
[51]Rendall 2005: 1.
[52]Rendall 2005.

as is done in the UK documents. This aligns with the political pressure from the broader civil rights organisations that expressed concern about a change in the question reducing the number of minoritised racial responses. In the case for both the Two or More analyses and the analyses of the six racial categories, there is discussion of both the racial group "alone" and the racial group "in combination."[53] For the purposes of the analyses, respondents are considered to be each of their racialised responses, in contrast to a completely new and separate racialised group, as conceptualised in the UK. Although the data are at times compared between the race alone and the race in combination categories, each major racial category can also be defined as the race "alone or in combination" group, which combines both sets of data. For example, in the article that overviews the Black population, it explains:

> [A] way to define the Black population is to combine those respondents who reported only Black with those who reported Black as well as one or more other races. [...] Another way to think of the Black *alone or in combination* population is the total number of people who identified entirely or partially as Black.[54]

A slight change in wording for the 2010 report says, "... total number of people who reported Black, whether or not they reported any other races."[55] The implication of racialisation being a summation of parts from the 2000 report was changed to speak only about how race was "reported"; a distancing from an official position based on racialised quanta. Nonetheless, the analyses were carried out in the same way for both census cycles. The US approach reflects a type of essentialising that constructs the Black population, as well as the others, as homogenisable by way of the same selected racialised category. Whilst this satisfies the concerns of the broader civil rights organisations, the wider implications of this essentialisation run counter to the wider social discourses around mixed-race identity and civil society, as explored further in Chapters 3 and 4.

Considering these two approaches, the two governments state different goals for their comparisons of mixed-race data to the other racialised groups categorised within each nation. In the case of the Mixed ethnicity data for the UK, the ONS states that one of their key issues of interest examines "... the extent to which [the Mixed ethnic groups] are more similar to the White group, or to the ethnic minority groups, from which they are drawn."[56] This particular wording appears to suggest a latent sense of binary essentialism in the government-defined ethnic categories, whilst at the same time, there is inconsistency with this assumption and the labelling of the groups as "new ethnicities." If the UK government understands the Mixed groups as new, the result would not necessarily be that the

---

[53]Jones and Bullock 2012; Jones and Smith 2001; McKinnon 2001.
[54]McKinnon 2001: 2, emphasis in original.
[55]Rastogi et al. 2011: 3.
[56]Bradford 2006: 3.

Mixed ethnic groups would either show similarities to the White majority group or to their specific or collective racially minoritised groups. Indeed, the ONS' analyses of the census data do not consistently show any similarities to one group over the other for any of the Mixed ethnicity groups, calling into question this assumptive approach.

The Two or More analyses in the US do not use language that stresses the comparisons between other racialised groups accounted for on Census 2000 or 2010. The reports on race are part of a series of reports that provide "portraits" of each racialised group, with regard to population, national distribution and housing data collected during each census cycle.[57] The reports describe the data for each racialised group (both alone and in combination, as well as a specific report for the Two or More races population) without comparing specific racialised categories. The Two or More races report does compare data between the general Two or More group and the general race alone groups, however the report refrains from doing so at a specific racialised group level. The reports also analyse data for race in conjunction with the data collected for Hispanic ethnicity. This is done by comparing the racialised group with no Hispanicity to the racialised group with Hispanicity. This compares ethnicity within the racialised classifications; however, the data are still considered to be for the same racialised group.

Mixed-Race: To Create or Not to Create a New Race Category

In both nations, then, the census bodies attempt to focus on what they likely consider an objective measurement of "race" and/or "ethnicity." Although on the surface, the censuses may seem similar in the US and the UK, the differences emerge quickly in the analyses of the data reports that each government publishes. Whilst the US had great public support and advocacy from mixed-race individuals and civil society organisations (CSOs) who campaigned for a mixed-race option on the 2000 census, and the US government acknowledged the importance in conceding to this change (on their terms), the official analyses are not detailed for the new Two or More population about which they claimed they were interested in finding out more. There is a much greater focus on the "race alone" groups than the Two or More races groups, and within the Two or More races groups, there is little focus on the different combinations represented by this larger category. Officially, the OMB does not acknowledge mixedness through the creation of a new category. This is reflective of the prevailing focus on separate and distinct racialised categories over the possibility of racialised mixture. As there remains no "mixed" category on the US census, reporting did not overtly reinforce commonalities or highlight distinctions among mixed-race populations. Rather, mixedness is constructed as a summation of racialised categories and analysed primarily alongside the singularly racialised groups. By adopting this strategy, the OMB does not create and reify new racialised categories. Instead, the strategy overlooks

---

[57]Jones and Bullock 2012; Jones and Smith 2001; McKinnon 2001.

potential trends for specific racialised mixes and reifies assumptions of hypodescent through analysing racialised categories "alone or in combination."

The generalised approach of the US census reports not only avoids creating new categories, but also falls short of generating detailed insights into specific areas of need and concern in the public reports that the race question might highlight. The approach taken by the US Census Bureau focussed on geographic analyses, opposed to specific analyses of the Two or More population. The analyses view mixed-race not as a cohesive group, but rather as a group that would display elements of any of the races one identifies with, as well as perhaps similarities with others who also identify into more than one racial category. With this approach, there is little that the census could illuminate about specific groups, as the respondents are rarely examined at the level of specific racial combinations.

The analysts of the UK Mixed ethnic data approach the mixed-race category in a different way from the US. There was not the same strong political effort from individuals and CSOs leading up to the 2001 census to allow for a mixed-race category on the census questionnaire. The government's consultation process primarily led them to add a Mixed ethnic category, comprising four subgroups of Mixed ethnicity based on the likely ethnic mixes present in the UK from since the 1950s. Since the Mixed ethnic population was described as a *group*, the UK government was able to use it as a variable and compare the data for the Mixed ethnic group with the other enumerated ethnic groups, as well as within the category at the subgroup level. The UK strategy suggests an acknowledgement of the ways different groups are racialised in the country, including potentially diverse implications within a general "Mixed" category. However, a tension remains in that by rigidly constructing mixedness into specific combinations of backgrounds and treating them as largely separate, the ONS does not only describe phenomena, but also acts to legitimate and reify these socially constructed groups that they have created. The census reports are consequently more detailed for the Mixed ethnic groups in the UK than they are for the Two or More population in the US. The UK government approached the Mixed ethnicity categories as an amalgamation of their racialised parts, so-to-speak; however, the data were not as straightforward as this prediction would suppose and found this hypothesis inaccurate.

From Category Construction to Category Usage

An individual's understandings of "race" and "ethnicity" will guide his/her/their decision(s) on which category or categories to select on the race or ethnicity question. Subsequently, the issue of how respondents interpret the census question has arisen to varying extents in both nations. When the ethnicity question was originally introduced to the UK census during the 1991 cycle, the ONS found unexpected responses for some of the ethnic categories. Richard Berthoud (1998) outlines that the results in 1991 revealed a conceptual dilemma as to whether the ethnicity question was meant to capture the concepts of ancestry or heritage, or whether it was to capture notions of identity and belonging. An example of this was seen when comparing the responses for Black ethnicity to the other ethnic categories. For example, responses for the Asian category tended to suggest that respondents understood their "ethnicity" to be related to their ancestral country or countries of origin. In contrast, responses for the Black category tended to align with a sense of national identity rather than ancestral heritage, particularly for those of Caribbean ancestry. Consequently, there were significant responses of "Black British" written in the Black Other category rather than using the provided Black Caribbean (or Black African, in rare instances) option to indicate familial region of origin. The subsequent censuses revised the category names to "Black or Black British" and "Asian or Asian British" in 2001, and then to "Black/African/Caribbean/Black British" and "Asian/Asian British" in 2011 to help address the identified ambiguities found in the 1991 census responses.[58] The shifting of terminology suggests that for the ONS, their conception of "ethnicity" is somehow the same or similar for a person born and raised, for example, in Africa, the Caribbean, or in the UK. This is despite the potential differences in language, cultural expression, nationality, and other aspects of socialisation that can comprise broader understandings of ethnicity. The linguistic changes aimed at consolidating such a diverse group of people into a single "ethnicity" – as the ONS views it – illuminate the racialised nature and purpose of the UK's ethnicity category.

Follow up research on the US census has identified comparable divergence between racialised ancestry and notions of personal or shared identity. For example, a majority of respondents (61 per cent) that have more than one racialised background indicated that they do not consider themselves to "be" (identify as) mixed-race.[59] As a reason for this, respondents indicated that they are viewed as being of one race by the general public; subsequently their sense of personal and/or shared identity is different from their ancestral racialisation. Thus, census responses reflect notions of identity as more personally significant than ancestry.

Conclusion

With the addition of mixed-race to the 2000 (US) and 2001 (UK) censuses, the census has become an important site to examine how the state officially constructs and recognises mixedness. Not only do the two censuses differ in their general terminologies for racialised differences, but the options given for self-identification – including mixed-race identification – are also specific for each nation.

The main findings of these analyses highlight the overall distinct ways that the US and the UK use discursive practices to conceptualise mixed-race. The censuses in both countries articulate constructions of mixed-race that subsequently shape the ways that the rest of each nation's institutions and population understand, accept, and/or contest mixed-race. The particular enumeration processes in each nation creates and defines categories. Racialisation further happens through the official discourses that they produce. The mixed-race categories are not mere descriptions of data, but are complex constructions carried out by the state for

---

[58]Berthoud 1998.
[59]Pew Research Center 2015.

the purposes of producing a racialised narrative of the population. Mixed-Race constructions are fraught with social meanings and consequences, which are then provided as a framework through which individuals are allowed to categorise and be officially recognised by the state.

Despite the lack of consistency in what constitutes a "race" or an "ethnicity," the way that the government agencies in the UK and the US describe race and ethnicity in these classification questions helps to uncover the general understandings and attitudes around race and ethnicity in each nation state. The census in the UK offers considerably fewer racialised options than the US census. The phenomenon of individuals having differential interpretation of official census categories further illuminates the fluidity and complexity of respondents' understandings of racialised categories. The next chapter thus turns to micro-level analyses that examine how individuals interpret, feel about, and engage with the census and its categories in the US and UK.

Chapter 3

Black, British Asian, Mixed-Race, or Jedi: Mixed-Race Identity in the US and UK

The study of identities is a foundational focus of academic disciples such as Sociology, Psychology, Social Psychology, and of interdisciplinary fields such as Critical Mixed Race Studies (CMRS). An "identity" refers to "the set of meanings that define who one is when one is an occupant of a particular role in society, a member of a particular group or claims particular characteristics that identify him or her as a unique person."[1] Regarding race, Roth (2016) defines racial identity as "a person's subjective self-understanding" and distinguishes this from other dimensions of race such as what racial categories one selects on forms, how one is racially classified by others, one's ancestry, and more.[2]

Whilst most members of society are socially ascribed to a racial group and thus have little agency in selecting their racial identity, some groups have more "ethnic options" or "flexible ethnicities" to identify as they please than others.[3] According to many CMRS scholars, mixed-race people constitute one such group who have a degree of "choice" in their racial identity.[4] Rockquemore's early work, for example, found that mixed-race individuals racially identify: with one race; with both races ("border" or "blended" identity); situationally as one or the other or both races ("protean" identity); or by rejecting group racial identification all together ("transcendent" racial identity).[5] Brunsma (2006) demonstrated the importance of context when his analyses of data from the US census and other national surveys showed regional variation in mixed-race identity.[6]

---

[1]Burke and Stets 2009: 3.
[2]Roth 2016, 2018.
[3]Vasquez 2010; Waters 1990.
[4]For example, Brunsma 2006; Davenport 2018; Rockquemore 1999; Root 1992; Song 2003.
[5]Rockquemore 1999; Brunsma and Rockquemore 2001; Rockquemore and Arend 2002.
[6]Brunsma 2006.

Mixed-Race in the US and UK: Comparing the Past, Present, and Future, 29–39
Copyright © 2020 by Jennifer Patrice Sims and Chinelo L. Njaka
Published under exclusive licence
doi:10.1108/978-1-78769-553-520191004

As explained in the previous chapter, one major similarity with regard to mixed-race identities in both the US and UK is the timing of the census changes to allow its recognition. Continuing from there, this chapter draws on interviews with 30 mixed-race adults in the US and UK to analyse the similarities and differences between how mixed-race people in both nations assert their identities (or not) on these forms. Mixed-Race people's perceptions of the racial options on the census and other official forms are first considered, followed by a discussion of two factors that influence their identity in the two nations: the differential influence of the "one-drop rule" and the differential intersection of nationality and race.

Black, British Asian, Mixed-Race, or Jedi: Indicating Identity on Bureaucratic Forms

The US and UK censuses' previous mono-racial identity categories were perfectly fine for some mixed-race people but were a source of great annoyance for others. Lisa (40, UK, Black/White) is an example of someone who held the former view. Prior to 2001 when the UK instituted a mixed ethnicity box, Lisa recalls that she "always chose Black …. It would have been nice to have more choice but I wasn't unhappy choosing Black. It was fine." In the US, a "Mark one or more" census format was implemented in 2000 in lieu of a standalone mixed-race category, but not all official data collection forms adopted it. Aaliyah (25, US, Black/White) explains that she has no issues marking Black "if I'm checking forms and they don't have a check all that apply sort of thing." Anna (24, US, Asian/White) "would always check the Asian or Asian American box. Korean, if that was it." Marking only one race category did not upset these interviewees. None of them expressed feeling like they were being forced to misrepresent their identity or to deny a parent or part of their heritage.

Other interviewees, however, enthusiastically welcomed the 2000/2001 change that enabled mixed-race identification. Heather (25, US, Asian/Black) previously marked "other" on forms, but she did not like it. She explains: "I feel so oppressed with 'other.' I feel like a creature or something." Mark (49, US, Native American/White) also dislikes when forms ask for only one race saying:

> If it is the case where it's like, no, you have to pick one. It's like, okay, fine, I'll choose Native American. And I always feel as though I've sort of lopped off an arm in the process of doing that. It's kind of like, why do I have to do that? So if I have the opportunity to check more than one box, that's exactly what I do.

In the UK, Claire (40, UK, Asian/White) views the new data collection techniques as reflecting the UK having "sort of caught up to the twenty-first century." Others appreciate it because they saw the old format as a source of stress. Dave (30, UK, Black/White) remembers that filling out forms "was always a bit of a 'damn what do I write.' Usually click, tick 'other,' and write in underneath 'Black White' and 'Black Caribbean.'" Sara (38, UK, Black/White) also greatly prefers the new format, saying "I mean now there is a box on the forms for mixed-race so I just tick that; but before it was a bit of a nightmare having to put 'other.'"

The UK's new box did not end the "nightmare" for all mixed-race people, though. Multiple UK interviewees pointed out that there were problematic assumptions built into the category. Sara explained that:

> [W]hen they have mixed, they have White with everything. But they don't have Black and Asian as mixed, which I always think is a bit weird. Yeah, it's assuming that everybody who's mixed is gonna be half White, but that's a load of crap really because if you're Chinese Black what do you put? So they really, it's a bit of an obvious oversight.

George (41, UK, Asian/Black) is one such double minority who is affected by this bureaucratic oversight. Of Indian and Jamaican heritage, George ticked a mono-racial Black box on his most recent census, in part because he identifies as Black and in part because there is no Asian/Black category to select.

Another issue is that in the UK "Asian" is assumed to refer to South Asian, for example, to Indian. This is problematic for Smith (25, UK, Asian/White) who has Chinese and Irish heritage. Reflecting on filling out forms he says that:

> There's never really an option for what I really am, you know. It's either, you can be mixed-race White and Asian but that implies mixed-race White and Indian in this country. I always select that box and people get surprised if I get called for interviews and things.

Whilst Smith ticks the Asian/White box despite the knowing the assumptions therein, Dean (27, UK, Black/White) does not tick the Black/White box because of his awareness of what that implies. As Sara noted, mixed-race is assumed to be half-White; but Dean has one quarter White ancestry because his mother is Black/White mixed-race and his father was Black. Dean was raised by his mother and White grandmother because his father "wasn't really there" in the beginning and then "he died when I was about five." Nonetheless, he does not tick the new Black/White box, explaining that:

> It's not like I'm saying I'm not part White, it's like where do you draw the line? And I know mixed-race people really mean half White half Black .... And you know I'm not half White so that's why .... But obviously, technically I am mixed-race, but in a broader sense.

Despite assumptions that mixed-race means "half" White, Sophie (22, UK, Black/White) has no qualms asserting a mixed-race identity despite not meeting this unspoken criteria either. Like Dean, her mother is Black/White mixed-race, but her father is White rather than Black. Sophie made no mention of anything like "knowing mixed-race people really mean half White half Black" in her interview. She also did not express any concerns over ticking the Black/White box on forms.

The assumption that corresponds to the UK's various mixed ethnicity categories, therefore, appears to be that the person has half *or less* of the listed non-White ancestry. The UK census did not previously have categories such as mulatto, quadroon, or octoroon as the US census did; however, like those twentieth century US terms for (Black/White) mixed-race people, the current UK options insinuate half or majority White ancestry with a little non-White ancestry. Given that no boxes, in the US historically or the UK contemporarily, exist for multiple racial minority ancestries, "mixing" is thus principally constructed with Whiteness centred. Returning to the census options in the UK, this underlying White-centered view of what it means to be mixed-race constrains some individuals' (e.g. George and Dean) ticking options just as the previous mono-racial identification format did.

Whilst the US "mark one or more" format alleviates the oversights and assumptive issues that interviewees expressed regarding the UK categories, it did not address the situation of some mixed-race people holding a philosophical stance against providing their race on forms at all. For instance, Frost (28, US, Black/Latino[7]) identifies as Black but does not mark that on forms. He explains that "I usually type in 'other' and put 'human being' to be honest with you." This began "probably around high school. But it might have been sooner than that" and was influenced by his father who is "African American but he's a practicing Buddhist and more interested in oneness and unity as opposed to separation. So he started doing that and I picked up on it." Annette's (31, US, Black/White) father, who is White, went even further. He does not fill out racial questions on forms at all. Regarding the census, she told the following story:

> My dad has never been sort of approving of people asking nosy questions. So he's one of those people like "this is the number of people in the household. That's what you're constitutionally allowed to ask. Don't bother me." I know that when I – I guess it was the '90 census, I guess he got a call from one of their enumerators. And he basically said "I don't want to be bothered with this." And I guess they left him alone. When 2000 came, um that was kind of funny because you know I'm hearing all about, okay, now you can check off more than one race and everything. And I knew that my dad was just going to do what he did for the '90 census. I didn't really bother him about it.

---

[7]As described in the previous chapter, Hispanic/Latino is considered an "ethnicity" versus a race in the US currently; however, two-thirds of Hispanics/Latinos in the US consider it a part of their race (Pew Research Center 2015). Advertisements for Sims' research only mentioned "race," but when people who considered Latino/Hispanic heritage part of their race volunteered to participate, they were included.

As Frost's father influenced the way he fills out forms, so too did Annette's father influence her adult behaviour. Whilst she identifies as mixed-race, Annette nonetheless "got in the habit of clicking 'refuse to answer' a lot" on forms.

Of the UK interviewees, only Sara expressed any reluctance to fill out forms in general or the census in particular. Discussing the latter, she states that "I don't fill in the census ... Um, I don't like the government to basically track me. I'm pretty anti-state so I don't really agree with it." Sophie estimates that due to these kinds of sentiments "null point two of our population are technically Jedi[8] according to the census. It's like 'I don't care, this is so stupid, fuck the government man.'" These practices are, on the one hand, evidence of mixed-race people and others exercising agency with regard to how they are classified. On the other hand, though, since census and other demographic data facilitate recognising, addressing, and preventing group based racial discrimination, including discrimination against mixed-race people,[9] asserting individual agency in this particular manner suggests at best a lack of awareness and at worst a lack of concern that census and other data are used for social justice efforts.

Though their box ticking patterns may not always match it, the mixed-race people in this sample had a variety of ways of understanding their racial identity. In addition to the influence of currently available tick boxes on their censuses, interviewees' racial identity was influenced by White supremacist norms of hypo-descent and by colonialist notions of racialised nationality.

"Black is Black": The Differential Influence of the "One-Drop Rule"

Given both nations' history of African enslavement, both the US and UK are cultures in which perception via hypodescent, that is, the "one-drop" of Black blood makes one Black "rule," is routinely applied to people of African descent. It should not be particularly surprising therefore that interviewees with Black heritage expressed and felt that they had fewer racial identity options than others. Across both national contexts, half (11 of 23) of Black mixed-race interviewees identified mono-racially as Black. In contrast, of the seven interviewees with no Black ancestry only one person, Sally (19, US, Asian/White) who identifies as "Filipino," identified mono-racially. This points to the differential strength of norms by hypodescent for persons with Black ancestry compared to others as demonstrated elsewhere.[10]

---

[8] According to the Office for National Statistics, on the 2001 UK Census over 300,000 people wrote in Jedi to indicate their religion. This represented about 0.7 per cent of the total population of England and Wales. The number of Jedi decreased by almost half in 2011, leading Robert Booth (2012) to quip in *The Guardian* that "the force is apparently on the wane" in the nation.

[9] Hernández 2018.

[10] Davenport 2018.

Supporting this interpretation of the numbers are the Black identified mixed-race interviewees' explanations for their singular Black identity. Bo (36, US, Black/White) was most explicit, saying "I am considered Black and having one drop of African American blood in you makes you Black." Others agreed, describing how peers viewed them as Black regardless of their mixed-race heritage. In discussing why he identifies as Black, Larell (22, US, Black/White) told stories such as the following of times in high school when he "was trying to find myself" and would experiment with asserting different identities:

> I was a sales associate [at Aldo shoe store] for a while. And yeah, I said I was Caucasian. And they called me back for the interview. And, I mean, I got the job and everything. I mean, after working there for maybe two or three weeks, the [white woman] manager, who I was obviously cool with by then, straight up told me. She was like, "Hey, I'm not gonna lie, when I saw your application, I thought you were White. Why'd you put that?" And I was like, "Because I am." And the manager's like, "But you're Black." And then I'm like, "Well, I'm half White and half Black." "Well, yeah, but like, shouldn't you just put Black?" It was kind of like, I mean, I didn't take offense to it but, I mean, it kind of made me think. She's right. There's been other situations where it's kind of awkward if a mixed person just claims the White side or something. It's like, clearly Black. That's how everybody, I feel like, looks at you. So I don't know. I thought that was funny. I was like, "I can't be White?" She was like, "No, it's cool."

From these and other experiences Larell concluded that "If I put White, I'm looked at as like, dude, you're not even White." In contrast, if he marks Black "it's accepted that I'm Black. 'Oh yeah, you're Black. Cool. Oh, you're mixed? You're mixed with White too? Okay. That's cool. But you're still Black.'"

Experimental research corroborates Larell's experiences. Using a self-identified Black/White mixed-race man's photo that had been pre-tested and found to be racially ambiguous, Stockstill (2018) varied his asserted race (either Black, mixed, multiracial, or White) on a mock job application and asked business students in the US to recall various information from the application. Two-thirds of study participants in the White identity assertion condition refused to accept the man's White identity. Some incorrectly stated that the man's race had not been listed on the application. Others incorrectly recalled that his race was listed as Black/African American. Written comments such as "Marked as White on employee sheets but looked a little Black" and "White on the application not in the picture" demonstrate that when others perceive one as Black assertions of membership in different racial categories are not accepted.[11] Mills (2017) characterises both Stockstill's study participants and Larell's former boss as engaged in "malevolent border patrolling," that is, the practice of relocating a mixed-race person to a racial

---

[11]Stockstill 2018: 135.

group other than the one(s) they indicated "primarily based on the appearance of the multiracial person and the strangers' perception of them."[12] As Larell's case and other research studies[13] have shown, these experiences have a profound impact on racial identity.

Only US interviewees are quoted thus far because 60 per cent of US interviewees with African ancestry mono-racially identified as Black compared to only 25 per cent[14] of UK interviewees with African ancestry. As UK CMRS scholars have noted, a "less stringent 'one-drop' rule seems to have operated in Britain."[15] Interviewees mentioned this explicitly. For example, although Dave was perceived as Black in predominantly white Yorkshire, upon moving to London he learned that most people in that multicultural global city did not perceived him as Black. During his interview, he expressed a desire to move to the US because he assumed that even in large diverse US cities he would experience "just kinda essentially being seen as Black, just light skin." Dean has family in both the US and UK and confirms this differential perception. In discussing why he thinks he is more frequently asked "what race are you?"/"where are you from?" in the UK versus the US, he said he feels that he is perceived as Black, "just light skin" as Dave put it, in the US. He explained: "America, because of like the history and that and the one-drop thing, like Black is Black. You know, like Mariah Carey is Black [in the US] so (laughs). We don't have that here, you know." In explicitly drawing on the one-drop rule in the US to discuss the perception of Black mixed-race people in the UK, these interviewees show how their understanding of mixed-race racialisation is "tied to extra- and trans-territorial conceptions and expressions."[16] In short, whilst notions of hypodescent differ in the two nations, they are relational in that their perceived strength is understood through comparison with the other.

Whilst it is evident that the one-drop rule appears to be laxly applied to light skinned mixed-race men like Dave and Dean in the UK, darker skinned men of Black heritage also experience less automatic racial assignment to Black in that nation as well. Vincent (36, UK, Black/White), for example, is a dark brown skinned man from Yorkshire. He mentioned that, were friends to describe him, they would likely say " 'oh, you know Vince, black Vince.' 'Oh, I know black Vince.' " Nevertheless, he feels that this is not a hypodescent-based ascription to the mono-racial Black racial category but that his friends are simply "describing you in this literal sense. To use a coarse definition: 'Oh, you know Jim. Fat Jim.' 'Oh, right.' People would describe in very literal terms." Whether or not Vincent's friends mean "black" in the "literal" sense of the colour or they mean "Black" in the sense of seeing him as mono-racially Black versus mixed-race is debatable,

---

[12]Mills 2017: 103.

[13]Khanna 2004; Khanna and Johnson 2010; Sims 2016.

[14]Whilst 25 per cent may seem small and in fact represents only two UK interviewees, as will be noted later in the chapter it is nonetheless higher than the *zero* per cent of non-Black UK interviewees who identified monoracially.

[15]Song and Aspinall 2012: 6.

[16]Goldberg 2009: 1273.

especially given that Dave grew up in the same area and does feel like he was racialised as Black. However, the fact that the men disagree and that Vincent does not feel like his peers are applying the one-drop rule to him further demonstrates the weaker nature of this ideology in the UK context.

Although the number of Black mixed-race UK interviewees who identified mono-racially in part due to the influence of the one-drop rule is small, it is nonetheless higher than the zero per cent of non-Black UK interviewees who identified mono-racially. Thus, whilst the one-drop rule may be weaker overall in the UK than in the US, in both nations it is comparatively stronger for mixed-race people of African descent than for mixed-race people other heritages. In sum, norms of hypodescent, that is, the infamous "one-drop rule," do not exert the same amount of influence in both places or for all races.

"Londoner Does Not Equal White": The Intersection of National Identity and Race

Whilst the norm of hypodescented minority identity was stronger in the US, racialised national identity was stronger in the UK. Claire for instance credits her lifelong "half White, half Asian" racial identity in part to the national pride that was instilled in her as a child:

> I mean, I think I've always felt I was half White, half Asian you know. Well, half Welsh. Because I think growing up in Wales it's one thing that you do get a sense of is the Welsh is very proud of their identity. They're not British. They describe themselves as Welsh. So yeah, I still think of myself as half Welsh, half Sri Lankan.

Other UK interviewees similarly discussed nationality and race as intricately linked. In answering the question of what was his racial identity, for example, Smith reports that "I always identify myself as mixed-race White and Chinese. I'd say I was British though." Including that he considers himself British in his answer to a question about his race demonstrates how he understands nationality as an embedded element of race.

The additive "though" on the end of his statement is noteworthy, however. Whilst Smith sees himself as British, others often do not. This is because in general "British," and even more so "English," is racialised as White.[17] Married couple

---

[17]Leddy-Owen (2014) interviewed an ethnically diverse group of 60 Londoners about their feelings of "Englishness" and found that across races it was discussed in essentialised terms and said or implied that only Whites were (seen as) "proper" English. As Leddy-Owen concludes, "ultimately their appearance to many within society as not White marks them out as non-English. Therefore, for these participants their non-Whiteness makes their experience of English identity precarious" (1456). Regarding Britishness, many of the mixed-race parents interviewed by Song (2017) were raising their second- and third-generation mixed-race children with a "British" identity. Racially,

Mary (41, UK, Asian/White) and George made this point clearly during the post-interview conversation:

> George: Uh, would you say that that Black person is British or English? They would say no.
> Mary: They would say no, yeah. 'cause for many people British or English equals White.
> George: That's it, that's it. Not Black, not Ind-, not Asian.

Mary revealed that "Londoner" was more salient for her than English or British because "Londoner could be literally anything, absolutely anything because it's a guess because it's not a national identity. It's very specific." Most importantly Mary prefers identifying as a Londoner because "Londoner does not equal White." Her husband concurs, adding:

> I grew up in London, now I'm in south London, but I was in east London and that's all I've known, you know, and that's how, that's what I feel. I don't feel British at all I feel London, that's it.

Whilst all of the UK interviewees were presently living in London at the time of their interview, 10 of the 12 were raised elsewhere; and with the sole exception of Smith, they strongly preferred their regional or country-specific identification to considering themselves "British." Vincent, as previously mentioned, grew up in Yorkshire in northern England where there is a strong regional identity, history, and culture distinct from central and southern England. Despite living in London, he still identifies as "I'm a Yorkshireman." However, he adds that "People don't think I'm a Yorkshireman." In other words, the regional identity of Yorkshiremen, like Mary and George noted of national identities such as English and British, is raced as White. Vincent's identity as a Yorkshireman thus is subject to malevolent border patrolling since it is seen as contradictory due to his non-White appearance.

Sara experiences malevolent border patrolling of her national identity, too. She grew up in southern England with "all English influence" due to her Jamaican father's absence from the family. As an adult, she gets frustrated when people refuse to accept her Englishness, for example, by asking whether she and her parents were born in England. She rhetorically asks:

> Why do you need to know where my ancestors 500 years ago came from? It's not important. I mean, historically they are something to do with me; but the way I behave, I'm English. It's nothing to do with me really. I've never been [to Jamaica]. I don't live with them, so why do you need to know just 'cause I have different colour skin.

---

this included some who were imparting a mainly White British identity as well as those who saw British identity as a cosmopolitan identity that explicitly included mixedness.

By "different colour skin" Sara means not unambiguously white; and Anglo-Saxon white, moreover, because her "Spanish" or "olive" skin colour is light but not sufficiently "white" for automatic inclusion in Englishness. Like Vincent, Sara identifies culturally with the place of her birth and upbringing; but as those locations are racialised as White, their physical appearance makes receiving validation of their identities more difficult than it is for, say, Vincent's fraternal twin brother who is phenotypically Anglo-Saxon "white."

Whether half-Welsh, Londoner, Yorkshireman, Englishwoman, or British Asian racial identities in the UK were expressed in tandem with national and regional identities (precarious and otherwise). In the US, however, despite some interviewees using terms like African American or Native American, no one discussed their racial identity as connected to US American nationality or regionality. Californians, such as Larell and Sally, did express intense pride in and identification with their home state; but they gave no evidence that this was tied to how they identified racially or that US national, regional, or state affiliations were racialised one way or another. Moreover, despite research indicating that US American identity is consistently raced as White,[18] no US interviewees mentioned having their nationality challenged or invalidated due to their race,[19] not even the three interviewees with Asian heritage who might have been predicted to experience being seen as "forever foreigners."[20]

The immigration histories of the two nations could explain this difference. Native Americans, Africans, Asians, Mexicans, and more have all been in North America in large numbers before and since the first US colonies, but it is only since large-scale immigration post-World War II that a sizeable number of non-Whites have settled in the UK.[21] This means that US notions of racial difference

---

[18]Devos and Banaji 2005.

[19]In July of 2019, US President Donald Trump tweeted that four Congresswomen of colour should "go back and help fix the totally broken and crime infested places from which they came." The fact that all four Congresswomen are US citizens and three were born in the US reflects a "well-worn" xenophobic and nativist sentiment that has existed in the nation since "the dawn of the republic" (Rogers 2019). From Jefferson's idea to send some slaves back to Africa in the 1700s, to Asian Exclusion in the 1800s, to backlash against each successive immigrant group in the twentieth century, to present efforts to deport refugees and asylum seekers, the US has a long history of constructing those who are not White Anglo Saxon Protestant as an intruding "other." In the wake of Trump's tweets, *The New York Times* reported that more than 4,800 people wrote in to share their experiences with being told to "go back" (Rogers 2019). Nevertheless, none of the mixed-race US interviewees in this sample, nor any of the UK interviewees who had visited the US, reported having this experience. This suggests that, at least for mixed-race people, their racialisation is understood as intrinsic more than place-based, though it also may be a result of the time period of data collection since all interviews were conducted in 2011 and 2012, that is, right before the post-2016 resurgence of blatantly open expressions of White nationalism.

[20]Tuan 1998.

[21]Alibhai-Brown 2001. This different immigration history is also evident when looking

developed vis-à-vis internal diversity from settler colonialism, domestic slavery, and immigration in the nineteenth and early twentieth centuries, whilst the geographical separation between the British Isles and overseas colonies meant that understandings of racial difference in the UK developed vis-à-vis external diversity and the formation of modern nation-states. This could explain why US interviewees being asked about their racial identity did not mention any national, regional, or state-based identities, and why UK interviewees being asked about their racial identity prominently included them.

Conclusion

In sum, despite the recent census changes, mixed-race people in the US and UK still have concerns over how (or whether) to record their racial identities on forms. Inconsistent adoption across the US means that the former mono-racial format is often still in place on some non-census forms; and a personal dislike of race data collection in general means that some US mixed-race people refrain from providing information on their race regardless of question format. Moreover, the continued functioning of the "one-drop" rule, in both nations but more so in the US, means that despite the new option to "mark one or more" many mixed-race people in the US continue to "mark only one." In the UK, White dominant assumptions about mixedness mean that double minorities like George are still constructed as "other," and mixed-race people like Dean who have more minority heritage than White heritage feel uncomfortable or unable to identify as mixed-race at all.

Despite these issues, though, many mixed-race people are pleased that forced mono-racial identification, for the most part, is a relic of forms past. They think that it is "really important to specify what your multi races are" as Heather said. As the next chapter demonstrates, these types of quotidian ideas about the meaning and importance of mixed-race stem from the work of various civil society organisations.

---

at the immigrant generation of the interviewees. Whilst only four of the 18 (i.e. one in five) US interviewees were second- or third-generation immigrants, every single one of the UK interviewees was the child or grandchild of an immigrant.

Chapter 4

Mixed-Race Civil Society: Racial Paradigms and Mixed-Race (Re)production in the US and UK

> Denise: ... [A] mixed-race or multiracial individual [is] someone who is of two or more distinct racial groups.
> Xavier: [Mixed is] ... something you feel or you don't.

The above quotes represent two viewpoints, each from a different mixed-race civil society organisation (CSO). The positions convey the vastly divergent constructions of mixed-race among mixed-race CSOs in the US and the UK. Denise (US) defines mixed-race in a precise manner that relies on an assumption of objectivity to distinguish who falls into multiple categories and who does not. The contrasting quote from Xavier (UK) expresses a subjective construction of mixed-race that does not rely explicitly on categorisation, but rather on criteria left vague, intuitive, and determined by aspects of personal choice.

What is reflected at the heart of these quotes are the different ways that mixed-race can be and is being constructed within organisational practices. "Mixed-Race" is a concept that seems relatively certain to a particular representative or organisation (even in its subjectivity, in the second example). However, notions of mixed-race are shaped by historical and social influences and yield varying ideas over time and in different spaces. This is the case even among groups that organise around the common nomenclature of "mixed-race," as will be examined in this chapter.

Mixed-Race CSOs[1] in both nations vary in aims and goals. These CSOs aim to create relationships and notions of social identity among people who identify as mixed-race. Whilst some organisations have that as their primary end, others build upon social identity towards further goals. Some organisations have explicitly

---

[1]The full profiles of the mixed-race CSOs, including overviews of what each does and the specific people each work with, can be found in the Methodological Appendix.

Mixed-Race in the US and UK: Comparing the Past, Present, and Future, 41–63
Copyright © 2020 by Jennifer Patrice Sims and Chinelo L. Njaka
Published under exclusive licence
doi:10.1108/978-1-78769-553-520191005

political aims and therefore mobilise campaigns for their desired categorisation and advocate for representation at government levels. Some provide moral and/or material support through meetings, courses, and training aimed towards individuals racialised as mixed, whereas others use the internet and social media to disseminate information and promote collective identity. Although on a lesser scale and through different mechanisms to the census bodies discussed in Chapter 2, mixed-race CSOs are also examples of influential bodies that set themselves out as representatives to create and promote their own racialised notions of mixed-race. In their work of advocacy, campaigning, familial and social support, and education; a few individuals take on the role of the leadership of many, towards a "unified position." As Michele Elam (2011: 8) notes, mixed-race CSOs put forth claims on behalf of mixed-race individuals:

> Such organizations claim to be representative of and responsible to a larger number of people eager and poised to be identified and rallied. In that sense, the community they are trying to reach, to whom they are beholden, is as much a construction as a discovery.

In a similar manner to the census bodies, mixed-race CSOs are also constructing notions of mixed-race through influencing practices of defining the racialised groups that they purport to represent, as well as creating a collective voice or position for them. However, unlike census bodies that are responsible solely to the state, mixed-race CSOs have a different relationship with those being represented.

Engagement between mixed-race CSOs and state organisations developed during the late 1990s. In the US around the time of the 1990 census, a small number of mixed-race CSOs primarily from the US West coast (where the US Office of Management and Budget [OMB] has identified a large population of mixedness[2]) either formed or adjusted their strategy to lobby for the addition of a mixed-race category to the census. Although some of these organisations had been active since the late 1970s or early 1980s, these did not originally form with a political advocacy agenda. This came later, in response to the US census.[3] In the UK around this time, the same response was not obvious: mixed-race CSOs were emerging but were not active on the same political scale as the groups in the US. Following the 1991 census in the UK, the UK Office for National Statistics (ONS) was concerned about the number of census respondents who used the write-in option to indicate some form of racialised mixedness, and therefore could not straightforwardly be recoded for their purposes.[4] These concerns drove the inclusion of mixed-race categories in the 2001 census, but mixed-race CSOs were not directly consulted about these changes.[5] Mixed-Race civil society proliferated in both nations throughout the 2000s, but unlike those in the US, CSOs in the UK

---

[2]Njaka 2013b.
[3]DaCosta 2007; Williams 2006.
[4]Owen 2001.
[5]Owen 2001.

were not organised around specific changes to the UK census. Rather, they had more varied and less explicit political advocacy agenda.

Contemporary social movements have been defined by their focus on the "right to identity."[6] For mixed-race civil society, the struggle for the right to identity has led to contesting the social meaning of race as previously imposed by government bodies. This contestation is important in the process of forming race.[7] As set forth by the frameworks used by Kimberly McClain DaCosta (2007) and Doug McAdam et al. (1996), US mixed-race civil society's grievances with the structure of the census meet the first criterion for a social movement to emerge. The lobbying activity of these groups illustrates their expectation that they may be able to redress their grievances, meeting the second criterion. According to DaCosta (2007: 209):

> Grievances develop in a broader cultural context, so finding out why movements emerge requires looking at more than just the visible aspects of collective action such as organizations, protests, and conscious framings. It also requires that we look at the not-yet-politicized networks in which new social identities incubate. . . .

These analyses include both CSOs with an explicit political agenda (a primary goal of legislative campaigning) and those with implicit or no political agenda, in order to capture a range of stages of "incubation" of their constructions of mixed-race social identity.

The ways that mixed-race civil society is constructing mixed-race in both nations are analysed below. As racial projects, mixed-race CSOs are sites of the discursive (re)production of race.[8] The substance of these (re)productions is highlighted through the ways that representatives of the CSOs speak about race and mixed-race. These analyses identify the racialised paradigms through which the CSOs understand and formulate mixed-race in their mission, aims, and work. Understanding this further clarifies the fundamental ways that mixed-race is conceptualised and operationalised by the CSOs, how that is reflected in the work they do, and ultimately how that influences their relationship and interactions with the larger society.

Constructing Mixed-Race

The chapter examines how the nuances of the CSO representatives' "common sense" constructions of mixed-race inform the mixed-race constructions presented to the wider society.[9] The analyses focus on two elements of construction: the descriptions and conceptions of race used to explain "what race is," and the

---

[6]Cohen 1985; DaCosta 2007; Omi and Winant 1994.
[7]Omi and Winant 1994, 2015.
[8]Caballero 2004; Elam 2011; Sexton 2008; Spencer 2011.
[9]Essed 1991; Glasgow 2009.

paradigms through which they are developed. This section discusses the findings in three subsections: biological notions of race, limited social constructionist paradigms and post-race paradigms that aim to "do away with race" via mixed-race projects.

Race: "A Subgroup of the Human Race"

The first (pseudo-)scientific theories developed by various academic disciplines and institutions over the last few centuries to understand race were based on biological paradigms.[10] Even though social and other academic sciences have widely refuted biological constructions more recently,[11] aspects of biological notions are still drawn upon in non-academic lay paradigms of race.[12]

Biological paradigms of race are most obviously prevalent among the CSOs based in the US. However, the ways that biological theories are operationalised for constructing mixed-race varies from CSO to CSO. Two sister CSOs that advocate for a mixed-race census category adopt similar, "objective" definitions of race. An example of this is a quote by Denise (US), who prefaces her articulation of mixed-race by explaining race more generally:

> Race or racial background refers to a sub-group of the human race possessing common physical or genetic characteristics. Race is determined by genetic similarities passed hereditarily. Race is perceived as permanent, although the way a person self-identifies their race(s) may change. Examples include White, Black, and Asian. Ethnicity or ethnic group refers to a specific social group sharing a unique cultural heritage. Two people can be of the same race (e.g. White), but be from different ethnic groups (e.g. White and Hispanic/Latino).

The meaning imbued within this articulation is similar to contemporary academic biological race paradigms that purport to differentiate population groups.[13] In a similar way to those who continue to study race in the present day with assumptions of "real" biological human variations and the aim to quantify/qualify them,[14] Denise cites phenotype, genotype, and heredity as her "markers" for racial classification. However, even at this level of racialised categorisation, Denise's criteria are rather specific regarding reference to "common characteristics," but she does not elaborate upon which races specific common characteristics would belong. Biological anthropologist John H. Relethford concludes that

---

[10]Banton 1998; Garner 2010; Relethford 1996, 2009.
[11]For example, Banton 1998; Essed and Goldberg 2002; Garner 2010; Glasgow 2009; Murji and Solomos 2005; Spencer 2011.
[12]Garner 2010; Glasgow 2009; Ifekwunigwe 2004; Mason 1999; Zack 2002.
[13]Relethford 1996, 2009.
[14]For example, Relethford 2009.

race described in this way may "crudely and imprecisely describe *real* variation."[15] Relethford and others in his field subscribe to biological human variations and classifications by these criteria; however even they are critical of this lack of specificity. He stresses that this particular usage may tend "to reify *incorrect* conceptions of human variation."[16]

Denise gives "White, Black, and Asian" as her examples of races, which are determined by her aforementioned cited criteria. She distinguished between phenotype ("physical") and genotype ("genetic"), which although closely related, have interesting distinctions when examined more closely. Phenotype refers to the physical or external appearances (e.g. skin colour, hair colour/texture, eye colour/shape, nose shape/size, etc.) of individuals as criteria for racial classification, whereas genotype refers to something "internal" – perhaps on the DNA level, or perhaps some idea of "blood quantum," hypodescent or parental lineage – that determines race for Denise and her organisational work.[17] There is no genetic testing within the remit of the CSO's work, so there is some cultural, social, historical, and/or colloquial element to her use of the terminology. Considering this, these suppositions fit within the idea of heredity, to which Denise also refers in her criteria for racial classification. Cultural, social, historical, and/or colloquial elements must work together when phenotype alone does not place individuals into an "obvious" racial category. In this case, race is something that is tied to genotype and phenotype, and is articulated as objective and fixed categories assigned by the state.

Moreover, the two sister CSOs appear to have adopted uncritically the US census racial categories. In explaining her definition of race, Denise uses "White, Black, and Asian," which are three of the official categories used on the US census.[18] She uses them as given and objective; there is no questioning or further explanation given as to what the racial terms may mean. This is further evidenced by her description of varying ethnicities, which she says could be "White and Hispanic/Latino." Although she previously described "White" as a type of race, in her example of ethnicity, she uses the racialised "White" as a contrast to the ethnic "Hispanic/Latino." Here, she tries to highlight that "Hispanic/Latino" is – officially at least – not racialised, but rather is viewed by her organisations (and the US Census Bureau) as a separate "ethnicity, which people of any race may have" (Denise). However, in the way she describes this, she is implicitly racialising Hispanicity by contrasting it to a racialised category as her two examples of "ethnicity."

Whilst a social constructionist approach to race is not generally applied by these organisations, an interesting nuance in what Denise says is that race *can* be social only inasmuch as the ways people may express their race(s). She says that *self*-identification may vary from time to time, notwithstanding an implied

---

[15]Relethford 2009: 20, emphasis added.
[16]Relethford 2009: 21, emphasis added.
[17]Bullock 2010; Spickard 1992.
[18]Grieco and Cassidy 2001.

"actual" race – the way a person is "perceived" – that remains fixed. In this paradigm, Denise links "perception" with the characteristics that distinguish human "subgroups," which are the (unspecified) external biological characteristics that she cites. Within this, she prioritises these external signifiers as those that determine her objective view of race, whilst allowing for some flexibility in the ways that people may identify themselves. Yet, self-identification does not alter the permanent nature of race. In this way, her word choice of "perceived" seems to allow for some subjectivity, though her descriptions of the ("actual") race that is perceived are, to her, objective and fixed.

For the two sister CSOs that adopt this racial paradigm, this has particular implications for the ways that they describe mixed-race and the specific work they do. For both, mixed-race is also something that is objective, which is illustrated by how Courtney (US) discusses mixed-race. She articulates, "I would define a mixed-race or multiracial individual as someone who is of two or more distinct racial groups. This would include children of multiracial parents." Considering the quotes from Denise and Courtney together, as racialised distinctions are discrete and externally assigned based primarily on physical or genetic criteria, "mixed-race" within their paradigm is having ancestry from more than one of these constructed racialised categories. For them, mixed-race identification – just as other racial categories – is neither influenced by personal experiences or other social contexts, nor by the ways individuals may view themselves. An example of this in operation would be if someone had parentage from more than one of their racialised categories, that he/she/they may consider himself/herself/themself to be of one race or mixed-race (or some other racial or non-racial designation entirely), but for the purposes of these organisations, the person *is* "mixed-race" by the "fact" of his/her/their parents' biological characteristics (and the racial groups into which those characteristics allocate them), as well as possibly the person's own.

This way of describing race is a relatively clear example of a contemporary biological race paradigm. In terms of racial classifications, the paradigm is articulated as being objective in nature, which means there is minimal room for individuals to have any input into how others see them. The hint of a social constructionist caveat offered by Denise does not extend that far; it only speaks to self-expressions that may change with circumstances. As such, race itself is described as something that is rigid in nature, as it is a specific identification that does not change.

Moreover, the racial categories cited are uncritically and unreflectively adopted from the US census and are treated as a matter-of-fact. In this way, these US organisations implicitly align their organisational views of race with the historical, socio-political views of race evidenced throughout the census. The census not only heavily relies on biological paradigms of race, but also developed a language to describe the different recognised races in the US that has gone unquestioned in the use of these organisations in their articulations of race. Where these CSOs do challenge the US Census Bureau is in the lack of official acknowledgement of people who have ancestry from two or more of the rigid categories developed by the OMB (and accepted by these organisations).

In the UK, there are also examples of biological race paradigms used by mixed-race CSOs. Xavier, who runs an educational support group to promote "positive" mixed-race discussion and identities for schoolchildren, gives an example of the specific demographic with which he works in his organisation:

> So, for example, some people might say that all Jamaicans are mixed-race, but I'm not talking about their actual heritage mix. I'm talking about a lived experience within the UK where one person will have a White and a non-White parent. But you could have a Black African and a Black Jamaican parent, but I wouldn't consider that child to be mixed-race because their experiences are both within the same racial group.

Relying on reified notions of racialisation, Xavier explicitly rejects historical or "multigenerational" racialised mixture as leading to what he calls the same "lived experience" that having two differently racialised parents does for people in the UK today. Interestingly, Xavier does not negate social elements of race completely; indeed, he cites "lived experience" as being an important part of racial identity in the above quote – and thus, inclusion as mixed-race. However, he is sceptical that different types of mixtures (e.g. multigenerational or official UK census subgroupings[19]) lead to similar or comparable "lived experiences" as those who are racialised as being mixed. Xavier added that "… [T]he students I come across are identifiably mixed-race, in that they do not have mono-heritage parents" (meaning two parents of the same race). Not only does he continue to stress his firm ideology of biological racialisation as an important signifier of the students with which he works, but also when describing some of his CSO's goals, he mentioned that one part was trying to increase "physical representation within schools" of "mixed-race identity" (Xavier). This aim is another example of the way that phenotype forms an important part of mixed-race definition for some organisations. For these organisations, representations of people who "look like me," is deemed important as a way of inclusion and acceptance. This idea of a mixed-race phenotype, however, may work to reify an idea of what a mixed-race person "looks like"; as when considering all the backgrounds that could possibly make up mixedness, the diversity in what these organisations are attempting to qualify is too wide to capture into a representative figure or two.

Xavier limits his operationalisation of mixed-race to those who have parents from two different racial groups; unambiguously stating the specific situation where one parent is White and the other is non-White. This is in line with UK census categories of mixedness, whereby all the specific Mixed ethnic subcategories

---

[19]The Ethnicity question on the 2001 England and Wales census offers five main ethnicity categories with subgroup options that additionally specify nation-, region-, or (in the case of *Mixed*) race-, or continent of ancestral origin. In the instance referred to by the interviewee for the main ethnic group *Black or Black British*, the subcategories offered are *Caribbean*, *African*, or *Any other Black background*.

include "White." Despite acknowledging what "some people" say about racialised mixture among Jamaicans or having parents who would be categorised under different subgroupings within an ethnicity category in the UK, Xavier states clearly that he does not consider that to be mixed-race. Presumably, for him, there is an external, "lived experience" distinction between people who have parents from different racialised categories (as Xavier defines them) and multigenerational racialised mixture, which may include mixture among census subcategories.

Xavier explains that this distinction is determined by a "lived experience" that is connected to having parents from two racialised groups. Xavier posits that this is something that is not experienced by people who have parents from different ethnicities or cultures that are still categorised as being in the same racialised group in the UK. For Xavier, just as "racial groups" are linked to biological differences, "lived experience" is also connected to biology. During the interview, he recalled that the young people in his organisation used "mixed-race" to describe their "experience from two parent[s'] different [races]." Again, "(lived) experience" is usually used as a social term, but in the case of this CSO, it is being "biologised" in that it is directly referring to components of biological race. It is not being used as a critique of biological notions of race or as a social constructionist approach to explore mixed-race. Rather, it is expressed as a rather objective feature that is definitive of mixed-race itself.

Similar to Xavier, Linda (UK), who also works to promote "positive" ("Black/White") mixed identity among other advocacy and community aims, appeals to a biological paradigm of race to articulate her specific definition of mixed-race. As she explains:

> [...] [F]or the purposes of trying to reach the people we want to reach, we see mixed-race as anybody who has parents from two different races. Not parents who are necessarily from two different countries; that is what I term as "dual heritage." But mixed-race is parents from two different races.

Linda distinguishes between the meaning she places on race and country of origin vis-à-vis mixture. Similarly to Xavier, she gives an example that excludes parentage from different countries that do not encompass racial differences as she constructs them. As she explores this further, she begins to make a distinction between aspects of difference based on origin and external – or phenotypic – differences.

> [...] I think "heritage" relates to property, that you're more or less inheriting something, and we do not, you know, as far as I'm concerned, "dual heritage" or, you know, "mixed heritage" can relate to people who are just from different countries or say somebody English who moves to America .... [T]hey've got their English heritage and they're now going to acquire a new one in America.

Linda does not seem to put the same social importance on the two distinctions as Xavier does. For her, what she is labelling "heritage" (a national and cultural label related to origin or residency) has a passive connotation that is merely something one "inherits." She uses this word to imply that the concept or label of "heritage" is passed down but has little social consequence. Likening it to "property"; it is as if she is comparing it to something that is concrete and stable, lifeless, and relatively taken for granted in the UK (and US) contexts.[20] It describes to a certain extent where a person may be from or where they may live, but it does not go much further than that. This type of conception for heritage does not encapsulate external appearances, and it does not describe cultural distinctions, either, from how Linda describes her perspective. Because of her perspective on the way she understands "heritage," she does not see the benefit of focussing on the mixture of heritage, as it does not specifically address the real issue, which for her is what she constructs as "race."

Linda returns to speaking specifically about phenotype as a marker for racialised difference. She draws upon her own phenotypic associations with Black mixture and she reflects that:

> [...] [P]eople treat you a certain way because you're going to look a certain way. You can be mixed in other ways and not look, you know, not particularly look like your, you know, non-European racial background, but if you are Black and White mix, you tend to have Black features or Black hair, etc., so people can identify quickly that you have some Black in you and people will then treat you in a certain way because of that.

Linda speaks somewhat generally and yet, still at times quite pointedly about phenotype and the ways that she associates it to different racial groups. Speaking generally, she asserts someone who she considers mixed-race may not "look like" they have a "non-European" background. However, appearances would only include the non-specified and assumed criteria used to distinguish biological race, which leaves them highly subjective in nature. On the other hand, when speaking about Black mixture and associated phenotypic markers (i.e. "Black features, Black hair, etc." as well as having "some Black in you"), the examples were specific and listed as though these aspects of "observed race"[21] were objective and uniform across all racialised Black populations. Within this particular application of the biological race paradigm, there is an internal incongruity, in that it claims to be objective in distinguishing racial categories, but the criteria for organising the racial categories are subjective, often unspecific, and based on assumptions.

In addition to phenotype as a way of understanding race, Linda also reflects explicitly and implicitly on "racism" as part of her constructions of race and mixed-race. Before the above portion of the interview, she emphatically states that, "[A]s far as I'm concerned, racism still exists and as long as racism exists, you can't get rid of the word 'race', because you always have to draw attention to it."

---

[20]Scott and Marshall 2009.
[21]Roth 2016.

Considering this context, a connection becomes clearer between her concerns about treatment based on phenotype and her constructions of race based on phenotype. She touches on the notion of (White) "passing"[22] for some of those constructed as mixed-race, but says that for those with Black mixture, it is more difficult because of the phenotypic associations she attaches to Black mixture. As such, racism will feature as part of the consequence for having specific sets of phenotypic characteristics, as they differ from those constructed to be part of the White racialised group. In this way, she links a type of social consequence (racism) to phenotypic differentiations as a way of supporting her biological racial paradigm.

Phenotype and racism are important themes around the biological construction of mixed-race for Linda. As she continues talking through the phenotypic implications of mixed-race and racism, she gives a more practical example of how this might affect someone she would define as mixed-race:

> [...] I think it's really important that when children are growing up that they have the influence of both races if they are mixed-race and this brings problems, you know? Say you've been brought up by one parent and that parent may not, they may not understand the importance of you having a balanced um, you know, cultural upbringing. So, for instance if your one parent is European and you only ever learn about the European culture and you don't learn about your, your other parent's culture, it, it won't really matter when you're very young, but as you start to get older and you start to, um, establish a sense of identity, you're going to come across problems, because society will always see you as a certain way. And, you know, if you have no ammunition, you have no tools to deal with, say racism, um, from both sides of your background, then it's going to cause you a lot of problems. [...] And, you know, it's not necessarily, you know, just a Black and White thing.

Here, Linda gives a reason why those that she constructs as racially mixed should have a cognizance of their mixedness. In her example she shifts between the ideas of culture and race, ultimately speaking about culture as race. She gives an example of a mixed-race child being brought up by a "European" parent. In the scenario, the child is only exposed to "European culture" and not the other parent's "culture." But, in fact, she is using "European" as a proxy word for the racialised concept of Whiteness. Within the context she is speaking, "European" has little specificity or meaning in terms of place of birth, language, dress, or other forms of common cultural markers. On the contrary, the term is being used as a homogenising stand-in for race, as referenced to at the beginning of the excerpt. Within this framing, Linda does not acknowledge the possibility for non-White

---

[22] "(White) Passing" usually refers to the attempt of a person of mixed ancestry to be accepted as part of a dominant white group, but other types of passing are possible, too" (Hernández-Campoy and Conde-Silvestre 2012: 357).

Europeans. When Linda begins to speak about "identity," it seems as if she could be speaking again about culture on the surface, but then she begins referencing physical appearance, racism, and ultimately race again; thus supporting that she likely was speaking about race all along. "Other" or "non-European" – in reference to parentage – are not any type of discernible cultural grouping. However, if she is speaking of race, this fits neatly into the common biological race binary of White/Other; or White/Black, which she points to at the end of the excerpt. When speaking about identity, she contrasts this with "society will always see you as a certain way"; a supposition which she problematises. Rather than this contrast inferring identity as a cultural process that includes many social elements, it limits it, in a literal way, to how a person is viewed: appearance, phenotype, and race.

Linda also makes a distinction between the mixture of race and other forms of mixture – in this case: nation of origin. This follows her focus on the salience of race in the UK and the importance of race for her particular organisation. For her, it is important to maintain a distinction between "race" and other forms of difference in background.

Neela (UK), in slight contrast, acknowledged an uncertainty in how she and her organisation conceptualise mixed-race, especially when starting her grassroots group to provide support to mixed-race individuals and families. Here, she describes the first pilot meeting of her group:

> [...] I think there were something like, about three Black dads and there were two sort of mixed-race dads, and then there was one Black father and then the rest were all, it was that kind of that breakdown. And actually, what we did discover and particularly face-to-face because at this stage, you've got to remember we were still naïve in our understanding of what mixed parentage was about or what our concept of how we felt, you know, mixed-race was.

For Neela, her work with the organisation she represents is a "journey," and this includes her own conceptions of mixed-race and the ones developed within the context of her CSO. It was the participants who showed up that helped to develop her ideas and conceptions of mixed-race. In this particular account, in addition to the racialised descriptions mentioned above, she goes on to describe a "White" family that also showed up to the first meeting. After asking them about why they were interested in attending the group meeting, they shared their mixed racial and ethnic backgrounds and subsequent experiences. As Neela described it, the mother in this family explained that although she appeared White, she had "African or [Asian] Indian blood in her." She and one of her siblings had been "very white" in skin tone and another sibling was "a light brown colour." She explained to the group that because of the different looks and experiences she had growing up within her family by people in the community, she was always conscious of her own mixed status. The mother further explained that her husband was White, and they had adopted children together with varying backgrounds and phenotypes, and they did not want their children to lose their identities either, especially when they looked "more White" and had parents who looked White.

The "journey" ethos, in terms of conceptualising mixed-race, allows for flexibility and fluidity as members attend and share their backgrounds and stories. One of the outcomes of the pilot meeting was noting who attended, what their backgrounds were, and why they were interested in the group. As the group continues to meet, Neela stresses that this pilot meeting helped to develop her own and the organisation's working definitions of mixed-race to extend to a concept that goes beyond obvious physical appearances and specific racialised categories. Nevertheless, the definitions and concepts remain still rooted in racialised language, even if the categories are broader than the official UK racial groups.

Relative subjectivity is another aspect of mixed-race operationalisation present in the interviews, in that mixed-race comes down to a sense of personal identity. Femilola (UK) also expressed that mixed-race is about "how people view themselves." Xavier (UK) speaks about mixed-race as "being something you feel or you don't." Interestingly, this seems in tension with his conceptions of mixed-race examined in above paragraphs. There, he linked mixed-race as being specific to racialisation (having a White parent and a non-White parent) and not inclusive of mixedness within racialised categories. However, some people may "feel" mixed-race with other types of mixed backgrounds, as expressed by some of the other respondents. They are not excluded from his work; therefore, on some level, Xavier must also allow for personal identification and "feeling" to be included in his operational usage of mixed-race.

In the operationalisation of mixed-race for the CSOs, there is generally more rigidity vis-à-vis conceptions of mixed-race found for the US organisations than for the organisations in the UK. Whilst the conceptions of mixed-race remained closely around "race" categories, some CSOs in the UK expand their understanding of biological mixed-race and relevant issues to those with other forms of mixed or multiple backgrounds, including having parentage from different nations, cultures and other forms of diversity, and notions of personal identification with mixedness.

Although on the surface, the mixed-race CSOs gave very similar answers to the question of "What is mixed-race?" it quickly becomes clear that beneath the surface, the organisations have different and distinct concepts of the term. An area where this is especially contentious concerns the notion of mixedness throughout generations, which is the idea of acknowledging racialised mixture beyond immediate parentage. This is significant because in more recent critical mixed-race theorisation, multigenerational mixedness has been a particular salient issue for criticising the constructions of mixedness by mixed-race civil society.

Holly (US) is part of a network that organises specifically and exclusively around "Black/White" mixed-race. The CSOs that she runs include an education and training group for parents of mixed-race children and a socialising network for mixed-race adults. In addition to mixed-race referring to having parentage of two different ("socially defined") races, she, unlike Xavier and Linda above, talks about "multigenerational" mixed-race. She defines this as "their parents are not of two different races. Maybe it's their grandparents or great grandparents."

Here, she specifically acknowledges mixedness through generations, which is not a common focus for mixed-race civil society or on surveys that ask for racialised classification from a list of official options. She does make a "distinction" to indicate that there is a difference in her mind about the identity and experience of multigenerational mixed-race from the identity and experience of a person who has parents from two or more different racialised categories. However, there is contradictory racialised logic in this distinction, as the parents in question who have mixed-race parents (the "grandparents" in her example) would then be mixed-race, by her own definition. As the CSOs in which Holly is involved primarily focus on "Black/White" mixedness, perhaps she assumes that the two mixed-race parents would be of the "same (mixed) race," as if they were not, the mixed-race ceases to be only multigenerational.

When examining it further, to her, there is even more nuance in multigenerational mixed-race around identity and familiarity with ethno-racial ancestry. To further explain, she added:

> I think there's a distinction .... [...] [I]t's very different than, "Well, you know, I'm claiming my Whiteness from somebody back when I don't know." Or, "I'm claiming my Blackness –" ... [O]r, what White people do: "I'm claiming my Native American –. Don't know what tribe or what ancestor, but hey, I'm Native American." You know? I would say, "You're a White boy." Right? But, people can identify the way they want to, that being said.

In her explanation, there is significance in knowing the specifics of one's racialised backgrounds in claiming a mixed identity, and great scepticism around those who "claim" a mixed background without knowing the specifics of their racialised heritages, let alone belonging to relevant communities. In her statement, she links the knowledge of one's background with his/her/their personal identity, lived experience, and racialised socialisation. There is assumption in her statement about the ancestral distance of the racialised mixing and hypodescent, in that a person can be categorised as one race when not much is known about ancestry some generations past. For her, mixed-race is not purely about background, but is tied into a conscious understanding about that background.

Holly then reiterates that "people can identify the way they want to." This seems contradictory to her criticisms of those who do not know the specifics of their racialised heritage who, regardless, acknowledge its presence in their assertions of racialised background. Whilst the assertion is not necessarily equivalent to personal identity, it does appear that Holly would not accept people comparable to her examples as multigenerational mixed-race, even if they identified as such. From what she has said, it is reasonable to conclude that identity as multigenerational mixed-race requires a knowledge and understanding of ancestry that has a fairly recent mixed-race lineage.

Courtney (US), from a group that advocates for a mixed-race category, also speaks about (multigenerational) mixed-race parentage as being inclusive in her conception of mixed-race. She explained, "I would define a mixed-race or multiracial individual as someone who is of two or more distinct racial groups. This would include children of multiracial parents." Courtney is less critical and nuanced in her ideas of race than other interviewees, and subsequently her conception of mixed-race, as she accepts the notion that there are objective and discrete racial categories. Her organisation is one that advocates for an additional racial category for mixed-race people, which makes her stance on multiracial parentage interesting, with regard to hypodescent. A child from two people from the proposed "Multiracial" racial category, according to Courtney, would fall into a paradox, as the child would not be "mixed-race" when considering her definition of having parents from two distinct racialised groups. However, at the same time, the child would be considered "Multiracial" because both parents are "Multiracial." For her, these distinctions do not consider life experience or cultural elements, and is a categorisation based on an assumed objectivity of race and the idea that "one is what one's parents are." In this way, Courtney and Holly are distinctive in their inclusions of mixed-race parentage and lineage despite them both acknowledging it as part of their mixed-race definitions.

Generally, there is a wider scope for notions of mixed-race among the organisations in the UK than in the US. There is considerable variety in the mixedness each CSO acknowledges in their conceptions of mixed-race. In a comparable way to her US counterparts discussed in the previous section, Jemima (UK) – who works with racially and ethnically diverse families in inner-city London – specifically includes mixed-race in past generations in her conception of mixed-race.

> I think the technical term is when you have two parents from different races … but that could be … first generation, [or the] next generation. I think it's a very muddy kind of issue, where you'll get some kinds of mixed-race … that will know actually where [they come from] completely.

Jemima exposes a limit to her definitions of mixed-race as she contrasts the "technical" terminology with how it is operationalised in her understanding and in her work with the CSO by including "next generation" in her definition.

When considering mixedness through generations, the CSOs in the US and UK that spoke about it diverged greatly in their constructions. In the US, the organisations were generally wary of it, in that they mentioned it as special cases. Courtney allows for the children of mixed-race parents to be included in her construction of mixed-race, though the question remains: how far in one's heritage would this apply? Contrary to Courtney's inclusivity as "also mixed-race," Holly makes a special distinction for what she calls "multigenerational" mixed-race, where she negates the mixedness of parentage or heritage further back in the lineage due to the potential experiences people may have with these circumstances. In the UK, generally the CSOs readily constructed broad views of mixedness that went beyond strictly recent and biologised racialisation.

Race is a social construction, but …

In addition to the previously outlined cases where race was being constructed in relatively straightforward biological paradigms, Trevor (US), who cultivates mixed-race communities in his civil society work, has a different way of understanding race through a paradigm that has social and biological elements. Unlike Denise, Courtney, Xavier, and Linda; Trevor rejects "race" as a contemporary terminology. When exploring race specifically, he explains:

> [...] [T]he keyword in there is "race." So, race is a social construct. It has no scientific basis, so if you buy into race, you buy into a social construct. ... [I]f we are talking about race, we are ... with an eye to the past .... [...] ... [Y]ou have to buy into the categories of race, which are sort of false to begin with. So, if you buy into those categories, mixed-race ... would mean ... an individual whose parents belong to different racial categories, as they've been artificially defined .... Um, that's sort of the strict interpretation of it. I think it's funny because "race" is pejorative and at the same time, it's the sort of "Yankee Doodle" effect.

At a superficial level, Trevor appears to reject race as a biological concept with his proclamation that "race is a social construct." With that phrase, he also negates the "truth" of race by dismissing it as being false and artificial. When he explains more what he means by that, he links the notion of "social construct" to the past.[23] When his organisation engages around race, he says that they do so "with an eye to the past" and that race has a "'Yankee Doodle' effect"; a US American reference that conjures up a colonial/early post-colonial US, and by associative context the lack of civil rights for racialised minorities of the time. Also within this context, race is "pejorative"; requiring external judgement and categorisation that may not reflect an individual's preferences. Whilst Trevor appears to be rejecting the notion of race in the present, he stops short of doing so in the past; his implication being that it played a more "real" role in society before.

Trevor also suggests that in addition to his associating it with the past, part of what makes race a "social construct" is that it does not have scientific merit. He has a different attitude when he speaks about "ethnicity." Taking more affinity to that word, Trevor describes his take on ethnicity:

> Ethnicity, I think, is a little bit more, um, legitimate or something? ... [R]ace is a construct; like, totally fake. Ethnicity is more based on things that you can actually back up with science or observation. Different cultural groupings, I guess. It's sort of tough; it's a complex topic. It's not easy to sort of pin it down. But it's sort of like the overlapping of genetic and cultural influences, that's sort of how you form ethnicity ....

Trevor declares a legitimacy to "ethnicity" that he does not find applicable to "race." In the way that he discusses "ethnicity" in direct contrast to "race," it

---

[23]Alluding to the significant racial history of the US, including slavery, segregation, internment, exclusion acts, and other forms of legalised and illegal discrimination.

appears as though he is able to do so largely by replacing the word "race" with "ethnicity," distinctive from his other US-based counterparts. The two words have different historical usages, which are reflected in the ways that Trevor speaks about them. For Trevor, "race" has connotations based in the past, whereas "ethnicity" has more contemporary relevance for him. Once the word "race" is shifted to "ethnicity," then Trevor easily describes an accepted concept that is partly based on biological notions of race that he appeared to be rejecting in his earlier narrative. Trevor illustrates a clear example of racialising ethnicity, by referencing "science" and "genetics," and linking them to culture.

Additionally, reiterated in the latter quotation, the concept of race for Trevor is a "social construct" – "totally fake" and has "no scientific basis." Yet, there is a contradiction in his approach to "legitimacy" vis-à-vis a sociological notion of *social construction* that would negate biological race paradigms. What legitimises "ethnicity" as a meaningful concept for Trevor is the way that he uses it to biologise and racialise groups via "science or observation" in ways that he denies "race" does in the present. By evoking science, observation, and genetics, he refers to similar methods used by the other CSOs in the previous section that also rely on biological racialisation to construct race and determine groupings based on their constructed criteria. Despite his uncertainty of the connotation in the questioning of the term as he explains it, Trevor does seem to have a clear idea of "ethnicity" as he employs elements of heritage (genetics and science) and culture (observation).

We are all a part of one big human mixed-race family ...

Generally, the mixed-race CSOs agreed on a definition of mixed-race as "having parents of two different races." However, there were cases in both the US and the UK where a few of the organisations expressed some scepticism around "race," and revealed a desire to move away from the term and/or the concept altogether. These views are the closest to a "post-race" paradigm discussed during the interviews. The views were expressed in two broad ways: either that all individuals belong to the "human race"/a singular community or that each individual has racialised mixture and therefore race is an irrelevant social categorisation. In a way, these two positions appear to come to a similar conclusion that race and the processes and outcomes of racialisations are social phenomena rather than biological ones. However, the nuances in the thoughts behind these perspectives show that they are indeed quite different from each other. Thus, the desired outcomes of putting forward such post-race positions within the mixed-race CSOs and the ways by which they arrive at them are important to examine further.

Beginning with Neela (UK), she expressed the dislike of hers and the members of her organisation of the idea of race:

> [...] [T]hrough a discussion that we had with the families ... the conversation or debate came up about ... the word "race," and a lot of families agreed that actually ... to be mixed-race means that you, you're kind of separating yourself from the human race, so-to-speak ... we're all part of the human race ....

She articulates somewhat of a critique that race – and the process of racialisation – is something that separates human beings (from being a singular "race"); in a sense, ascribing difference that is not actually there. Although she does not use the "social construct" terminology that some of the other interviewees do, her articulation perhaps goes further than the mere term to explain why racial categorisation does not sit well within her CSO. It also touches on the social elements behind race that do not make sense to the organisation. This perspective aligns with "colourblind" ideologies whereby in attempts to move beyond race, the social reality of racialised discrimination is downplayed or ignored.[24] As Neela's CSO focusses greatly on issues such as belonging and isolation, whilst utilising racialised language to describe themselves and others, this would suggest that this articulated notion of a unified human race is a form of idealisation.

Perhaps another perspective with similar meaning, but with different framing, is the way Trevor (US) chooses to speak about his CSO and its participants as part of a "multicultural community." Rejecting race as merely a "social construct," and proposing "ethnicity" as a term more "legitimate," he goes on to say:

> To us, culture is the most easiest or the most salient attribute, you know? It's a little bit more useful and kind of definable. Let's put it this way: say, we just screened [the 1991 film] Mississippi Masala and you know, the main character is Indian descent that grew up in Uganda, moved to the UK and moved to the US. [...] Most of the characters identify as Ugandan but they are not from Uganda, genetically speaking, so that's culture. It's an easier way to address that. But not [that] they don't have cultural attributes that came from India, too. You know what I mean? Ethnically, they are from India, culturally they are from India, Uganda, and then later in like UK, US. So our mission statement, we say that we are trying to build multicultural community. So to us, the idea of culture is ... one of the best ways to define the positive things that define us as human beings. [...] It has that flexibility built into it. You know, it's portable. It's transferable. [...] Culture is traditions and customs and stuff. [...] So, when we are saying multicultural community, we are saying that we're encouraging an exchange between cultures.

Instead of using colourblind rhetoric (e.g. "not seeing" race, ethnicity, or colour), Trevor uses "multicultural" as an attempt to move away from racialisation and ethnicity alone in order to capture an element of the lived experience that results from being part of various diverse and cultural communities. For Trevor, racialised designations fit into that, but the term "multicultural" goes beyond that to something more practical in his mind ("salient," "useful," and "definable"). When speaking about Mississippi Masala (a romantic drama about an Indian–Ugandan family that moves to the US, where the daughter falls in love with a

---

[24]Saad 2020.

Black man from the US South), he mentions that the family is not "genetically" Ugandan. This is another attempt to talk about race without employing the term; genetics (or biology in general) does not determine national origins or links. Trevor is making a tacit distinction between the family in the film and Ugandans with (Black) African ancestry. By labelling it as "culture," he reconciles their own asserted identities as something distinct from other Ugandans, yet still "valid" and in addition to other identities that may rely more prominently on racialised or ethnic labels. In contrast to US-based Denise and Courtney, who take a more restrictive stance on terminology, Trevor uses his "culture" terminology to articulate being more inclusive and open about mixedness.

Following his stance on multicultural community articulated above, elsewhere in the interview, Trevor refrains from using "multiethnic" to describe his CSO's communities, as he views the term as referring solely to how he's explained "ethnic background" – as one of national origin. He links the term in his mind to "multiracial relationships," which is not what he wants to convey with "multicultural community." For his CSO, "multiethnic" or "multiracial" relationships should not face obstacles by society, but they are not "pushing" or encouraging them in their work. By using "multicultural community," those people in partnerships across racialised designations are included among other forms of cultural diversity welcomed by the group.

Taking these points together, Trevor desires to shift from a focus solely on race and ethnicity. He suggests that "race" and "ethnicity" divide people into nations or specific types of relationships comprising specific categories of people, which he views despairingly. Instead, he wants to encourage a notion of community (singular) where all people are welcomed and encouraged to share their social differences within the context of a community. This is the opposite of strict colourblind ideology; differences are not obscured but are celebrated. In a way, the notion of a singular community of which all can be part is similar to Neela's thoughts that everyone belongs to the same human race. In both articulations, the negative repercussions of racialisation and racialised categories are negated for a sense of oneness – whether real or imagined. Though there is acknowledged room in Trevor's vision for social diversity within his community, just as there is articulated diversity within Neela's group, both are reluctant to focus on race – specifically the mixed-race and ethnicity around which their CSOs focus in these statements. In this way, they reflect elements of post-race paradigms that have "moved beyond race" as a salient category.[25]

Shifting now to the second post-race articulation, mixed-race is seen commonly by the respondents as something that everybody is, in the end. However, most of the time this articulation is an offhand comment that is followed incongruously by specific ideas of what "mixed-race" means for particular organisations in practice, both in the US and in the UK. One respondent speaks in notable contrast to this, however. Labelling the term as "socio-political," Graeme (US) begins by carefully acknowledging the role of census categories in his articulation

---

[25]Goldberg 2015; Mirza 2015; Neblett 2011; Wise 2010.

of mixed-race: "... [I]t depends on the country you're in, in the United States, it's anyone whose parents cross traditional Census Bureau categories." By citing the country and the Census Bureau as sources for racial categories, Graeme shows his consciousness of a link between the state and people in social processes. In particular, he knows the role that the state plays in designating racialised categories and the public's adoption of those categories as meaningful for themselves. This was unique in the interviews, as no other interviewee articulated a link to the state in his/her understanding of racial difference.

He continued sharing his personal perspective, which in turn informs the work of the CSO:

> Ultimately, we're all mixed-race. I think all these terms are socio-political, so you can throw them around forever if you want. It depends on the society. [...] ... [M]ost countries have, uh, single words for mixed-race anyway, so you don't need, uh, you know, a dual word for it. Because it is clear that until we get to a, uh, position where we don't discuss race ... we've got to do something. And the best thing to describe, in my mind, populations that we encounter is people with many different racial or many different ethnic backgrounds, that's multi – more than two – and it shows more than one.

Of all the CSOs interviewed, Graeme is the most vehement in his post-race position. In this case, he explains that his use of racial categories is a pragmatic one. He uses them out of a sense of necessity, but that usage neither reflects his personal nor organisational perspectives on mixed-race. The quote above begins by stating that everyone is "mixed-race," which assumes that everyone has ancestry that crosses US census racial classifications. This is a commonly held notion articulated by the US-based mixed-race CSOs and follows along generalised post-racial thinking. In contrast and taking it further, however, he argues the socially constructed nature of race, of which a post-race paradigm is also part. Yet, he gives examples from other nations on how they have taken to labelling populations that have been racialised as mixed, which he uses as examples to solve the mixed-race "problem." Having racial categories for different "official" mixes departs in logic from his earlier assertions that everyone is mixed-race. Nonetheless, throughout the interview, he speaks about ending public discourses on race, and here is no exception – ultimately, he sees the way forward on dealing with "race" is to move forward from it.

Within his denial of the salience or even existence of mixed-race (as a meaningful construction), and despite his explanation for the necessity of terminology until the "end of race," he often slips[26] into the use of racialised language. An example

---

[26]Jungmiwha Suk Bullock conceptualises "slippage" as the "commonplace and unquestioned ... discourse [that relies] on racial essentialism that seems to suggest that race – although a social construction – is biologically quantifiable for multiracial identified people" (Bullock 2010: 3).

of this can be seen at the end of the quote above, where he speaks of people with different racial or ethnic groups in a way where he is not problematising race, as he has done elsewhere in the interview. Indeed, he is using it in a rather straight-forward way, much like the way he opens the quote stating matter-of-factly that we are all mixed-race. This could be due the difficulty of speaking about the social concept or construction of mixed-race whilst either avoiding the language that is often used within common discourses, or without using cumbersome language to explain more approximately what one means every time a racialised concept is invoked.

There is tension throughout Graeme's accounts of mixed-race as he explores his post-race perspective. Whilst he is advocating for a paradigm of post-race that limits the focus on racialised discourse as a salient biological and eventually social concept, it is not clear that he completely dismisses race as either type of construction. His reliance on the "we're all mixed-race" foundation holds tension if he truly does not believe in racialised categories, as then "mixed-race" has no meaning, biological or otherwise. Instead of speaking more to that, he speaks about how in other countries, they have different labels for the same concept, which does work to challenge and disrupt the rigid categorical structures present in the US. But he stops short of negating these other terms as also being ones socially constructed for those specific states. Instead, he favours terms that do not rely on using a prefix that implies mixture to describe populations. In this example, the focus becomes no longer on problematising the social construction of mixed-race, but rather problematising the labels applied to people racialised as mixed-race (US).

Despite this tensions, Graeme's views are consistent with some post-race para-digms. In his summation of the persistent problem of race, he concludes:

> […] [Y]ou're probably going to kill me for this, but I think one of the reasons why we're so focused on race is we have what I call a "sociological view" of populations, and one of the sociological views is to put everything into these groups. And I advocate – and I think we're going to begin to do that – is to move more towards a "psychological view" of people. Back to the individual and back to what attributes does an individual have, including race. But not just race – so that we are all multifaceted and belong to a variety of groups, not just one. […] And I think we're slowly going to get to that because people are getting sick and tired of this notion of you're just categorizing this wonderful complex thing called the human being into one group. That makes no sense.

Graeme's "psychological view" of populations does not aim to eliminate the notion of race (thus further indicating that Graeme does not go so far as to deny biological race or argue that it is does not exist). Instead, he contrasts it to his notion of a "sociological view" of populations that positions race to be a primary essentialising social category at the expense of other types of social and individual groupings. Elsewhere in the interview, Graeme speaks of how a "psychological view" and the elimination of the focus on racial groups will help to shift advocacy to focus on "needs" not necessarily tied to the essence of being mixed-race.

Graeme's preference for his "psychological view" is similar to a post-race paradigm that allows for being "rooted in, but not restricted by" a socially constructed racialised group.[27] Touré Neblett's view allows for the acknowledgement of the social construction of mixed-race, in this case, but also advocates for other types of group identifications. However, Graeme's position is not identical to that set out by Neblett, because Graeme would eventually like to eliminate racial categorisation. As a pragmatic decision, Graeme articulates that he uses categories presently only because the state continues to use them. Thus, Graeme also has a post-race stance that overlaps with the argument that race no longer needs to exist. Graeme's post-race framework lies between these two positions.

Conclusion

The concept of "mixed-race" is constructed in varying ways by the different CSOs interviewed in the UK and the US. This reflects the ways that historical and social influences impact civil society in its understanding, describing, and conceptualising of race. At times, the different CSOs overlap in their articulations, whilst at others, they oppose and contradict each other.

Interviewees articulated their descriptions and conceptualisations of mixed-race in ways that corresponded to three race paradigms: biological, social, and post-race. No articulation fit firmly into just one theory, but rather pulled from more than one at different points. For Denise and Courtney (both from the US), who give clear articulations that are mostly biological in nature, there is some leeway articulated for those who can express their race "socially" in certain circumstances. Although not expressed in the same ways explicitly, most CSOs in the US followed in the same vein and tended to rely on biological notions of race. This is in spite of whether or not they acknowledge some social elements in their racial understandings. In the UK articulations, whilst both Xavier and Linda speak about favouring a type of biological mixedness as their target group, they engage with other types of mixedness and attempt to explain why they are not inclined to include those who do not have a "lived experience" of mixed-race – in other words, are not racialised as mixed, even if they may have racialised or other mixture in their ancestral lineage. Conversely, some CSOs express that mixed-race is down to how a person feels or personally identifies, without any other criteria. This perspective is social in nature, in that – in its articulation, at least – it does not rely on any biology to define racialised categories.

When race is articulated as a "social construct," the language that follows from the organisations is often biological. In his racialisation of the term "ethnicity," Trevor quite clearly speaks in biological terms about how it is scientific and observable. As other groups merely utter that race is a "social construct," Trevor shows that he does understand the concept of social construction to some extent

---

[27]Neblett 2011: 12.

in saying that race has no scientific basis. Yet, when he substitutes "ethnicity" for "race," he supports the biologised concept he attempts to negate.

The post-race perspectives share the idea that in some way, society has "moved on" from race, whether it be that all people should be seen as human beings, that race is an irrelevant categorisation, or that race can be acknowledged without definement. Even within these strands, biology is referenced both to identify participants as "mixed-race" and to refer to that from which society needs to move on. In the case of Graeme, he argues both for the end of racial categories and the acknowledgement of race as well as other social groupings. In both positions, as he is arguing for a movement beyond race, he relies on biological notions of race as a basis from which to move forward.

With some exception, mixed-race civil society in the US tended to rely upon biological and cultural notions to construct essences of mixed-race, even when they articulated a belief of social constructionism. CSOs based in the UK tended to approach mixed-race as a more fluid conception that is based on post-race ideas influenced by colourblind approaches. When comparing the difference in biological focus between the US and the UK, David Mason writes:

> A key reason for this difference of emphasis probably lies in the greater visibility of "race" as a political and administrative category in the United States. In this connection it clearly denotes phenotypical [*sic.*] difference and may well help to reinforce popular biological conceptions which the authors even of sociological texts feel the need to address.[28]

Here, he highlights academic writers, however this may extend also to mixed-race civil society, who – in the case of the interviewees – also may be either academics or educators themselves, or at least more familiar with scholarly and activism discourses than the general public. The political and administrative aspects of racialised categorisation in the US were present throughout the interviews with the US-based CSOs. This is especially apparent in the cases when CSOs worked specifically to advocate for administrative categories against political bodies, such as the US Census Bureau.

The converse of the Mason quote helps to explain why the UK CSOs may not have been as fixated on categorisation overall, thus allowing them to be more exploratory about their constructions of mixed-race. The two UK CSOs that had a focus on "Black/White" mixed-race (represented by Xavier and Linda) tended to rely on biological racialised paradigms more than the UK CSOs that focus on mixedness generally. Perhaps this makes sense, in that as there is some sense of specificity (particularly for the group run by Linda), some forms of criteria were articulated as the organisers spoke about their participants. These CSOs that relied on biological paradigms also were the ones that preferred "race" in their terminology, which for them implied biological (specifically racialised) requirements.

---

[28]Mason 1999: 21.

The remaining UK CSOs had a more fluid approach to mixed-race. This was reflected in their openness both towards group membership, as well as their own thinking about how they spoke about mixed-race as being more than firm, objective definitions based on biological race. They spoke of their scepticism of fixed labels and gave examples of group members who did not fit "traditional" ideas of mixed-race who also desired the same support/education/advocacy as those with "identifiable" racialised mixedness. For them, the fixed biological labels were too limiting for the purposes of their work, and found it more useful and practical to be more open to the people who opted-in to their services.

Despite the various strategies used to understand and articulate race, the underpinning of biologised and culturised understandings present throughout all the represented CSOs makes clear the pervasiveness of these long-rejected ideas. Understanding the ways in which mixed-race CSOs construct mixed-race is important because it helps to show the specific ways that racial paradigms are at work presently. It is one thing to read about the shifts of racial paradigms in scholarly literature, but as these analyses have shown the implementation of the paradigms is neither discrete nor straightforward.

The next chapter turns from examining mixed-race at the organisational level towards the everyday experiences of mixed-race individuals in the US and UK. Analysing the micro-level shifts the focus from representative constructions of mixedness and centres individual agency in describing what it means to be mixed-race in the US and UK.

Chapter 5

"Sometimes It's the First Thing People Ask": Daily Experiences of Mixedness in the US and UK

As noted in the Introduction, one strength of this book is the inclusion of per-spectives from both those with the social power to influence the construction of mixed-race at the structural level as well as those without such power who live with and/or challenge these constructions in their daily lives. In the previous chapter, we analysed the rhetorical frameworks used by those working in mixed-race civil society organisations (CSOs) in the US and UK. This chapter takes a step down from the discourse propagated by a core of influential social actors to focus on the concrete daily experiences that mixed-race people have in the US and UK. It examines the common experience of mixed-race people being questioned about their race with attention to the frequency, location, phrasing of racial questions and mixed-race people's responses. With regard to how race structures everyday encounters, the experiences herein suggest that despite lofty discourse, neither the US nor the UK have actually moved very far away from traditional Eurocentric views of race which centre Whiteness, construct non-Whites as other, and expect the latter to politely accommodate the logic of the former.

"What Are You" versus "Where Are You From": Questioning Ambiguity in the US and UK

Critical Mixed Race Studies (CMRS) research has demonstrated that a pervasive mixed-race experience includes being questioned about one's race.[1] As adults, about half of Sims' interviewees "often" receives questions about their race. When asked to recall the most recent occurrence of this experience, they gave examples ranging from the month before to the week before to earlier in the very day of the interview. Regarding the regularity with which people ask them, UK interviewees reported

---

[1]Mills 2017; Paragg 2017; Root 1992; Sims 2016.

Mixed-Race in the US and UK: Comparing the Past, Present, and Future, 65–77
Copyright © 2020 by Jennifer Patrice Sims and Chinelo L. Njaka
Published under exclusive licence
doi:10.1108/978-1-78769-553-520191006

being asked "quite a lot" or "quite a bit." Fleur (34, UK, Black/White) elaborated that, "It's not many weeks go past without me being asked that. At least once a week on average." US interviewees similarly recalled being asked "all the time."

Whilst the frequency is similar, the phrasing of the question differs by nation, and in so doing reveals differences in the social construction of race. In the US, people were asked "what (race) are you" whilst in the UK questions were phrased as "where are you from." As discussed in Chapter 3, the more recent achievement of a critical mass of racial and ethnic minorities in the UK – combined with the historical understanding of the "other" as being in a far off exotic place – appears to combine to construct race as place based. Thus, your race is where you are from. In the US, on the other hand, the long history of greater domestic diversity appears to have constructed race more as intrinsic to a person. Although some groups are racialised as "forever foreigners"[2] in the US, race in this nation appears understood as less about "where" people and their immediate generations of family are "from"[3] and more about "what" they essentially "are."

Another difference between the accounts of experiences with questioning in the two nations is that in the US "what (race) are you?" can be the first question a person receives at the start of a conversation. Sophie (22, UK, Black/White) explains that in the UK "it's probably on their mind from the beginning but people [are] quite sensitive now a days. They're not gonna wanna just say 'Oh hi, you're Sophie! Where you from?'" US interviewees, however, reported this exact scenario occurring frequently. When asked if people ask her what race she is, Tia (37, US, Black/Native American/White) responded, "Oh yeah. Right away. Sometimes it's the first thing people ask. Sometimes people I'm not even talking to will stop and go, 'I just really want to know, what race are you?'" Frost (28, US, Black/Latino[4]) described similar experiences, explaining that "what are you?" is "Usually one of the number one questions I get asked."

Interviewees felt that their racially ambiguous appearance is what drives others to ask questions about their race.[5] As noted in the Introduction, these questions reveal observers' racialised gaze and their attempt to resolve the crisis of meaning that their encounter with ambiguity has created. Paragg (2017) explains that in Canada "what are you"/"where are you from" questions are evidence of the operation of a racialised gaze that seeks to place non-White bodies "at the edge of the nation and/or to place them (put them in their place) within the nation."[6] When the racial cues that are commonly used within a context to interpret others racially are insufficient to reach a conclusion, for example, when a person has a "physical appearance that approximates more than one race,"[7] others' inability to place them in a racial category creates a crisis of racial meaning that many feel compelled to immediately resolve.

---

[2]Tuan 1998.
[3]See chapter 3 endnote 19 regarding notions of were US Americans are "from."
[4]See chapter 3 endnote 7 regarding the racialisation of Latino.
[5]See Sims 2016.
[6]Paragg 2017: 284.
[7]Mills 2017: 70.

"They'll Ask You That While You're Working?" Locations of Question Encounters

CMRS studies have found that mixed-race people are asked about their race "in practically every context they find themselves."[8] One main location of question encounters for the mixed-race people in this sample was at work. Judy (30, US, Black/White) remembers being asked about her race from the time she began working:

> [W]hen I was about eighteen years old. One of my first jobs. This woman sitting in the break room. And I had talked to her lots of times before. But she randomly asked me, she said "Are you mixed?"

Others discuss similar experiences. Mary (41, UK, Asian/White) is a teacher and her students ask. Smith (25, UK, Asian/White), a medical student who works as an extra in movies, was asked on set mere hours before his interview. Vincent (36, UK, Black/White), who works in book publishing, recalled a client asking him at a networking event. Heather (25, US, Asian/Black), a graduate student who works as a waitress, is asked by restaurant patrons, as was Anna (24, US, Asian/White) during her brief stint as a café barista. Larell (22, US, Black/White), an undergraduate student who works as a grocery store cashier, explains how these experiences unfold:

> Larell: So I work at Trader Joes .... People come in there all the time like, "Hey, what ethnicity are you? Like what are you mixed with?" Or, "Are you mixed?"
> Jenn: They'll ask you that while you're working?
> Larell: Yeah. Ringing them up. We'll just be talking and stuff, casual conversation just to, you know, keep the customer service appeal up. For my managers.[9] Just little small talk. And they'll ask me. Honestly, every time I go to work, I get asked at least once.

By contrast, interviewees in very high status occupations, such as Frost and Sydney (39, US, Black/White) who are physicians and Bo (36, US, Black/White) who is the manager of an internationally iconic venue in his city, are not asked as often, if at all, in the work place. Bo describes how people "give you that look like

---

[8]Paragg 2017: 278; see also Mills 2017.
[9]Larell characterised the purpose of his response to questions about his race at work as a part of "customer service" that he does "for my managers." This highlights an economic dimension of mixedness, that is, how mixedness can function as cultural capital in economic markets. Mahanti (2014: 245–246) reminds CMRS scholars that we should "pay closer attention to the way that social capital informs mixed-race and the ways in which mixedness fits into the racial capitalism."

'What race are you?' and 'Oh and you're the manager?' " but he says no one asks him any questions about his race at work. Sydney believes that her high status is the reason, explaining "[T]he position that I'm in as their physician, they don't feel a, maybe comfortable to ask me initially." In other words, whilst people may ask a barista like Anna or a retail employee like Larell what race they are upon first encounter, Sydney suggests that they do not ask a person in a higher status occupation, at least not initially.

Given the general social phenomenon of beliefs about status characteristics influencing social interactions,[10] whilst discomfort questioning a person of a higher status than oneself is certainly one explanation for this observed difference, experimental research suggests that another explanation is that mixed-race people in high status occupations are perceived as White. For example, Freeman et al. (2011) created facial morphs along a continuum of prototypical Black (dark skin, wide nose, and thick lips) to prototypical White (light skin, thin nose, and thin lips) and tasked 26 participants with clicking whether each face they were randomly presented was White or Black. The morphs were shown with either high status attire (a suit) or low status attire (a t-shirt and jacket). Results showed that participants were more likely to categorised morphs attired in a suit as White and morphs attired in a t-shirt and jacket as Black, and that this influence of a class status cue was more pronounced for the ambiguous morphs than those nearer to the prototypical poles.[11] Freeman et al.'s work thus suggests that part of the reason why light skinned mixed-race professionals like Sydney, Frost, and Bo are not asked about their race at work whilst service workers like Anna and Larell consistently are, may be class cues influencing racial perception.

In addition to their place of employment, half of interviewees also discussed being asked questions about their race during social activities including parties, dance clubs, pubs, bars, gatherings at friends' houses, sporting events, and weddings. Sally (19, US, Asian/White) explains that it is because these settings involve meeting and getting to know new people. She says that if she is "hanging out with my friends and they have some of their friends who I don't know, they're just like, 'What race are you?' " The same thing happens to Mary: "[W]ell anytime we're at a party of any sort, that, it usually comes up. I think generally it comes up, uh, when meeting stra – new people, it always comes up, somehow, within about half an hour."

After work and parties, retail stores are a third location that mixed-race US interviewees were asked about their race. One of Joy's (27, US, Black/White) earliest memories of questions about her race, directed to her mother because she was a child, occurred in a grocery store. She recalled: "I was probably like, maybe like four. I wasn't in kindergarten yet. But I remember we were visiting, we were in Denver, Colorado. And some woman stopped my mom to ask her about me." As an adult, Joy deals with fellow shoppers who "just, you know, start talking." Sales clerks engage in this practice as well. Anna recalls a recent

---

[10]For example, Berger et al. 1972.
[11]Freeman et al. 2011.

shopping trip to the clothing store The Gap with her brother during which "the saleswoman approached us and was like, 'Oh my gosh, are you guys Hapa?' " In total, the frequency and location of these kinds of experiences are evidence of others' ubiquitous racial gaze and disquiet with ambiguity.

"You're So Pretty": How to Ask About Mixed-Race Without Asking About Mixed-Race

Questions such as "what are you" in the US and "where are you from" in the UK are understood in their respective contexts to be referring to race. However, in both nations, interviewees mentioned others' frequent use of lead-ins, explanations, and code words during these encounters, too. In *Racism Without Racists* (2018[2003]), Bonilla-Silva defines colourblind semantic moves as verbal tactics designed to function as "discursive buffers" to protect the speaker when they say "something that is or could be interpreted as racist."[12] Wording strategies such as prefacing a comment with the declaration that one is not racist, referencing a "friend" of colour during one's remarks, and refusing to commit to an answer or feigning ignorance of the topic have "become standard fare of the post-civil rights racial discourse."[13]

Interviewees' accounts of their experiences being asked about their race are replete with their inquisitors' use of semantic moves. Sara's (38, UK, Black/White) exchanges with a man on a dating website are exemplary of asking about her race indirectly:

> I sent my picture to this guy and he sent a response back saying "Are you Brazilian" so I said "No I'm actually British" and then he's like "What are you," I'm like saying "I'm, you know, I'm a mixture," and he's like "What! Of what?"

Whilst at first this may seem like a question about her nationality, it is actually the semantic move of asking indirectly. As discussed elsewhere,[14] mixed-race people are frequently mistaken as being Latino/from South American countries. However, given the rhetoric of *mestizaje* and the known history of wider spread racial mixing in Brazil, asking if a person – who is on an English dating website, has a traditionally English name, and has a town in south England listed as her hometown – is "Brazilian" can be seen as an indirect way to ask what they are "mixed with." As shown in Sara's escalating exchange with the man, "what" her racial "mixture" is was in fact the information he was seeking but did not directly ask initially.

Another semantic move interviewees observed others using is to reference a mixed-race "friend." Joy reports that people say "'Oh, yeah, I have a

---

[12]Bonilla-Silva 2018[2003]: 81.
[13]Bonilla-Silva 2018[2003]: 81.
[14]Sims 2016.

friend that's half Black, half White'" after she answers their question about her race. People asking Annette's (31, US, Black/White) race follow up as well, saying " 'Oh, I know somebody.' Or 'I've seen somebody and you have a similar look.' Or 'You look to be mixed also.' " This drawing on an unnamed mixed-race "friend" or "somebody" the person purportedly knows or has seen echoes the references to an unnamed Black or Asian "best friend" that Bonilla-Silva found function as "rhetorical shields" during colourblind race talk.[15] The mixed-race version of the phrase being offered after asking about a person's race suggests to Joy that, "They kind of feel like they might need to explain a little bit."

A third semantic move is leading with a compliment. Whilst in Judy's experience White people "seem to be very abrupt," the rest of the interviewees in both the US and especially in the UK felt that educated, upper income, and/or White people are, as Frost puts it, "uncomfortable to ask upfront sometimes. And they're usually more slick about it." Their "slickness" involves "lead[ing] in with something maybe nice. To get to their question" according to Joy. Compliments such as "Oh, wow, you're so pretty," "I like your hair," and "Oh, you have really pretty eyes" immediately precede "can I ask you what you are?" "where are you from?" and "where did you get your eyes?" The protective use of indirectness, references to a mixed-race friend, and leading with compliments during "what are you"/"where are you from" encounters all demonstrate that some people are aware that asking a stranger their race violates the contemporary colourblind racial zeitgeist, common social norms of civil inattention,[16] or both. That they engage in linguistic gymnastics in order to ask *anyway* is evidence that race not only continues to be a master framework but also that many people see those who are unintelligible to them within that framework as responsible for explaining themselves.

"I'm Mixed" versus "Human Being, Punk!" Mixed-Race People Respond

Whether worded as "what are you," "where are you from," or "where did you get your pretty eyes from," interviewees know that the race(s) and/or countries of origin of their non-White ancestors is the information being sought. No interviewees in either nation felt that people ask these questions purposefully to be rude, however only about a third of the sample was unbothered by the questions. Smith explains that being asked his race "doesn't bother me … no one's ever asked me maliciously what I was." Jennifer (34, US, Black/White) likewise does not mind because "I've never been in a situation where it seemed rude or sort of intrusive to me." Neither Claire (40, UK, Asian/White), Carmen (31, US, Asian/Black/Latino/White), nor Sally are bothered by the questions either. All of these interviewees attribute the questions to others' benign curiosity. Larell, for

---

[15]Bonilla-Silva 2018[2003]: 81–82.
[16]Goffman 1967, 1971.

instance, says when asked his race "I just tell them. I smile. It's cool that they're interested in, you know, what I am. Obviously they're curious. So I just answer questions. It brings up good conversations." Mary too believes being asked her race is a good conversation starter. She is a social studies teacher and each year her students ask her where she is from when they discuss ethnicity. She says "it's always a positive."

Interviewees who were amenable to answering questions about their race reported usually replying with "I'm mixed." As Paragg (2017) found, mixed-race people also have "ready identity narratives," that is, "stock answers" that "reference origins, or 'how' their linage 'came together.' "[17] These responses are given, often in a seemingly rehearsed or "highly performative" manner, when others inevitably ask their race; and they highlight the "constant presence of the external gaze in respondents' lives."[18] Analyzing these stock responses, Paragg finds that many of them "narrative to the expectation of the gaze and its need to know the originary [*sic.*] point of racial mixing."[19]

On the one hand, within the context of societies that have traditionally constructed races as mutually exclusive, responding with one's multiple heritages can be seen as asserting agency by making mixed-race heritage visible and legitimate.[20] On the other hand, when mixed-race people like Claire or Larell respond to strangers that they are "mixed-race half Welsh half Sri Lankan" and "mixed-race Black White," respectively, their words fulfil the expectation of the gaze. Therefore, though they may personally enjoy the conversation, they are nonetheless contributing to legitimising the racial gaze, the ideologies that construct their bodies as ambiguous, and the practice of questioning those who do not fit into dominant constructions of race.

Cazeneva (2015) describes such language as linguistic racial accommodation, which he defines as:

> the choice of words, concepts, phrases, and other language by individuals and organizations, including those of racially oppressed groups, that align their racial attitudes, behavior, and aspirations with the prevailing racial ideologies, practices, and sanctions of the dominant racialized group.[21]

In the US and UK, language that accommodates Whites' fragility – for example, the expectation that language will and should make Whites comfortable – is the prevailing semantic practice.[22] Even though interviewees reported that sometimes it was other people of colour who asked them what race they are, the

[17]Paragg 2017: 285.
[18]Paragg 2017: 285; Mathews 2007.
[19]Paragg 2017: 293.
[20]Mills 2017: 95.
[21]Cazenave 2015: 23.
[22]Bonilla-Silva 2018[2003]; Cazenave 2015; DiAngelo 2018.

racial ideology underpinning the question itself stems from hegemonic White supremacist obsession with racial difference. As Cazenave notes "systems of oppression flourish when the language that camouflages their ideological core is accepted as a given and therefore goes both unexamined and unchallenged."[23]

In contrast to linguistic racial accommodation, linguistic racial confrontation is language which *rejects* the ideological common sense of the dominant group and speaks "truth to power," a necessary step towards dismantling racist systems according to Cazenave. The majority of Sims' interviewees rejected the idea that it was acceptable for a complete stranger to ask about someone's race simply because they (the questioner) had no ill intent. Instead, these interviewees considered the questions "kind of rude" and "annoying." Aaliyah (25, US, Black/White) chronicles how she used to be okay with people's questions when she was younger, but now as an adult, they have become wearisome:

> I mean I think when I'm younger I would just say "I'm Black and White" and it wouldn't bother me as much. But over time it's definitely been annoying I guess ... it's just, it's just, more of like a hassle than anything. It's not like I go home and I'm depressed because someone asked me what race I am. But it's just, like, frustrating I guess.

Chris (30, US, Black/White) finds being asked about his race frustrating as well. Rejecting the dominant racial gaze, he asserts that "It's one of those questions that's unnecessary. Why does it matter?" Judy and Suzie (33, US, Black/White) agree, both rhetorically asking a hypothetical questioner "Why do you care?" The answer that hangs in the air is "to put you in the pigeon hole" according to Sara.

These interviewees' references to questions about their race being unnecessary and not something that others should care about underscore how the contemporary public places such as stores where they are asked are understood as "cosmopolitan canopies." Anderson (2004) describes a cosmopolitan canopy as a "heterogeneous and densely populated bounded public space" in cities where "a diversity of people can feel comfortable enough to relax their guard and go about their business more casually."[24] People are cordial and polite, and supposedly unencumbered by thoughts of race; but when race is brought to the forefront of an interaction, it reveals it all to be a façade. Writing with the example of a Black person, Anderson says these moments cause the person to realise:

> that some of his colleagues are not who they pretend to be. The situation becomes unavoidably racial. At that transformative

---

[23]Cazenave 2015: 2.
[24]Anderson 2004:15.

moment, the Black person discovers that he or she is utterly unequal, not accepted as normal but racially circumscribed.[25]

Anderson calls this a "Nigger moment." In so naming, he does not mean that a person is called a slur or experiences something as explicitly racist as being called "Nigger." He uses this infamous slur, however, as "a metaphor for outcaste status." Any time an outcaste status – minority status by race, class, gender, ability, etc. – is brought to the fore, it disrupts the illusion of egalitarian cosmopolitanism and colourblindness.[26]

For many mixed-race people, the experience of being asked about their race in public by a stranger is this type of moment. Contrary to the purported definition of cosmopolitan public spaces as neutral, they are reminded that in White supremacist societies others can actually be viewing them in explicitly racialised terms at any time. Being asked "what (race) are you"/"where are you from?" abruptly reinforces to mixed-race people that they are *not* perceived equally as just another person or shopper. They are perceived, first and foremost, in an ambiguously racialised manner.

Paragg (2017) found that whilst some mixed-race people narrated to the gaze in their responses at these times, others attempted to "unfix and expose the operation of race discourse."[27] This behaviour was evident among Sims' interviewees who disliked being asked about their race. They responded by either withholding the desired information or by asking a return question, sometimes quite forcefully, that delegitimised the initial question and its underlying logic and practice. Sara offers as an illustration the following exchange she had with a woman whilst on holiday in Turkey:

> She says to me "Where are you from" and I said "England" and then she said "Were you born there" and you know that's a racially [*sic.*] question wasn't it. Whenever I'm abroad people say "Were you born there."

As previously discussed, one explanation for the question being phrased "where are you from" in the UK/Europe versus "what (race) are you?" as in the US is the different immigration histories. Sara drew on this when she continued that the only reason people inquire further when she says she's English is "because I'm not White …. They think that everybody [with] brown skin has immigrated in the last five years or something." Considering her detailed racial ancestry "not important" to casual conversations, she frequently attempts to withhold the information and answers, truthfully, that yes she was born in England.

Lisa (40, UK, Black/White), too, withholds the information being sought when she responds to racial queries at home and abroad. When she is asked her

---

[25]Anderson 2011: 262.
[26]Anderson 2011: 271–272.
[27]Paragg 2017: 293.

race she replies simply with "African." Like Sara, she gives this answer knowing full well that it is not what the person asking her really wants to know. She
describes the digging that ensues:

> I got drilled a bit more, "Oh but you're not, really?" Even, I went
> to Kenya and it was like, "African." It's like "Yes, I am, actu-
> ally." And then some of them would guess. And others would say
> "Really? Come on now." And it's like yeah. And I wouldn't give
> them any help. So evil. I was like, what do you want me to do? So I
> would say "African." Um, and that's, yeah. I would get "Both your
> parents?" And I would say "No, only one." So yeah.

After years of experience with these questions, mixed-race people like Sara,
Lisa, and others are able to distinguish between people who ask their race to genu-
inely get to know them and those who are racially objectifying them. Demonstrat-
ing what Joseph-Salisbury (2018) calls "post-racial resilience,"[28] interviewees not
only identify and weather these difficult moments but a few go a step further to
respond strategically in order to convey to the person questioning them that their
query is problematic. For instance, when Fleur is asked "where are you from"
she responds with a return question of "[I]n terms of where do I live? Or where
are my parents from?" Whilst a portion of this is her attempt to "consider what
the person is really asking and response accordingly,"[29] she is usually sure they
mean the latter. She asks anyway, though, in order to make a point. She explains:

> Sometimes it's to make people think, do you actually know what
> you're asking me? And, I guess it's a kind of a defense kind of thing,
> really, in some way. Because it's kind of making somebody real-
> ize they're actually asking a quite personal question and I'm not
> going to kind of make it easy for them by giving them an answer
> straight away. It's almost like I want them to kind of acknowledge
> that they are asking something that's quite personal. And usually
> it makes them feel quite uncomfortable as well. Which is good.
> Because I think they should feel uncomfortable about asking a
> question like that to somebody they've never met before.

US interviewees withhold information and ask questions to make a point
as well; however, in line with the stereotype of US Americans as quite brusque,
they reported doing so more confrontationally than UK interviewees reported.
Aaliyah sometimes responds with "Does it matter?" Tia responds with what
she calls "sassy" remarks like "Human. A person." Frost takes it a step further
and responds to "what are you" with "Human being, punk! What you are?" Tia,
too, sometimes turns "what are you" back upon the person who asked her. US

---

[28] Joseph-Salisbury 2018: 17.
[29] Thompson 2000b: 173.

interviewees' purpose, like their UK counterparts', is to hold the person account-able for their unwelcome and (in their view) unwarranted racialised gaze.

Desmond and Emirbayer (2016[2010]) point out that asking questions is a powerful response to verbalisations of racist beliefs[30]; and whilst there can be debate as to whether or not asking someone "what are you"/"where are you from" is evidence of harbouring racist beliefs, it is clear that responding with a question reveals the racially othering assumptions that underpin the initial query. Whether the person answers aloud or not, the assumptions behind their question are exposed when they are directly challenged. Aaliyah's response of "Does it matter" forces people to consider why, in the middle of a dinner party, knowing the race of the person eating fish tacos matters. Tia and Frost turning the question around and posing it back to their inquisitor throws into sharp relief that all people, including the questioner, are actually racialised.

In sum, what the dominant logic characterises as "sassy" is in fact linguistic racial confrontation[31] as it challenges the legitimacy of the current racial practice. By responding to questions about their race in a manner that "makes [the ques-tioner] feel quite uncomfortable," mixed-race people "do race" in a way that chal-lenges the established racial ideology which constructs some bodies as ambiguous and subject to random inquisition from strangers. According to Tia, her sassy responses are effective, as evidenced by others backtracking and apologising with comments like "'Oh, I'm sorry, I didn't mean to be rude.'" In short, by respond-ing to "what are you"/"where are you from" differently than expected, mixed-race people challenge hegemonic understanding of (mixed-)race and contribute to (re)constructing it in contemporary society.

"That's Actually How I Met Suzie": Empathetic Asking and the Building of Mixed-Race Solidarity

The majority of the sample expressed negative feelings towards being asked "what are you?"/"where are you from," from Mark (49, US, Native American/White) who finds it mildly annoying that he has to "explain myself again and again" to Heather who strongly stated "I hate that question." It is consistent, then, that two-thirds of the interviewees do not ask other people these questions. Judy explains that she asks others about their race "rarely" and adds that "It has to be like, you have to just be puzzling the hell out of me for me to ask."

Nevertheless, a third of the sample did admit to more than rarely asking oth-ers the very same questions that many of them so disliked. Claire says she has "a curiosity as well about, of people … And I'm interested in, you know, finding out where they're from and what their mix is." Suzie claims to have "mixed people radar" and says "I'm not going to lie … I'll be like, 'Are you mixed?'" Moreover, mixed-race people recognise the irony in asking other people's race given their own feelings on the questions. Chris, when asked if he ever asks other people what

---

[30]Desmond and Emirbayer 2016[2010]: 413.
[31]Cazenave 2015.

race they are, revealed "that's actually how I met Suzie ... I guess I'm guilty too." Dave laughs that "it's quite funny 'cause as mixed-people, as it were, we hate this question yet it's sort of the first thing we ask one another."

Interviewees feel that it is qualitatively different, however, when another mixed-race person asks their race. Fleur describes feeling "an affinity with that person because I know they've probably been asked that question lots of times. And it's almost like a, you know, bonding thing really." Dave describes how it is "not a kinda probe. You're not kinda constructed in a, I don't know, some kind of fetishistic way. It's more empathic." In the US, Heather phrases it as wanting to "feel that sense of connection" with other mixed-race people whilst Aaliyah and Larell explicitly describe a mixed-race "solidarity." Discussing the disproportionate number of women compared to men who ask about his race, for example, Larell says it would be "weird"[32] if a man asked unless the man were also mixed-race. In that case, Larell says "it's kind of like a mixed power thing. 'Hey, what are you? Mixed? I knew it man. I'm mixed too.' 'Yeah we got this, bro.' "

Sims has discussed elsewhere how being asked "what are you"/"where are you from" and having other experiences being consistently inconsistently perceived is "apparently understood to be a quintessentially mixed-race experience."[33] In that vein, these experiences appear to not only serve as reflected appraisals of mixed-race identity but also as a common bonding experience with similarly situated others as well. Supporting this is the fact that many interviewees discussed important close and long-term relationships that they have developed with other mixed-race people. Suzie and Chris met at a party of a mutual friend and have remained friends. Aaliyah's and Tia's[34] closest friends in high school were other

---

[32]Although fewer men reported being frequently asked about their race than women, half of them recalled that women asked noticeably more often than men. Larell and Frost both responded "definitely women" when asked which gender questions them the most. Whilst Dave feels a bit racially "vetted" (see Buggs 2017b) when women ask, Chris represents the other men when he speculates that women are "just making conversation." Nevertheless, Larell explains that he would feel awkward having that conversation with another man saying that "Like if it actually happened face to face, man to man, it would be like 'Why are you so interested in what I'm mixed with, bro?' " As will be discussed in chapter 7, race, gender, and sexuality combine to not only influence perceptions of mixed-race people but their social experiences within the heterosexual matrix as well (Butler 1990). With regard to gender norms for conversations about race, therefore, it appears that in the US and UK it is more acceptable to ask racial questions cross gender than within gender. Perhaps questions about race, since they reveal having paid close attention to someone's body, convey potential sexual interest in the other person. This would explain why in heteronormative societies like the US and UK men pose the question more often to women than to other men, and it is "definitely women" who ask men the most.

[33]Sims 2016: 579.

[34]Tia's mixed-race friends group identity was so strong that all members acquired matching tattoos to commemorate their bond (discussed in Sims 2018).

mixed-race girls. That Mary and George are married, and the friendship group of their two children contains many mixed-race children, including one who's "mum and dad are more or less the same mix as us," is even stronger testament to the experience of "mixed-race solidary" about which some interviewees spoke.

Conclusion

Being asked questions such as "What are you?" and "Where are you from?" are a routine part of life for many mixed-race people in both the US and UK. Whether at work, on a dating ap, or whilst shopping, others' racial gaze attempts to "place" them with the dominant racial framework; and people will ask for assistance when they unable to do so. The timing and phrasing of these racialised questions differs somewhat by context, though, with racailised inquiries occurring earlier in conversations in the US and with discursive buffers and other semantic moves being quite common especially in the UK. Whilst some mixed-race people are unbothered by such questions and answer them freely, others consider them annoying, unnecessary, and rude. When mixed-race people respond with "sassy" remarks such as "Does it matter" or forcefully declare "Human being, punk!" they "do race" differently than expected and in so doing challenge the legitimacy of the racial gaze as well as White supremacist valuation and constructions of race.

The fact that some mixed-race people bond and form strong friendships, even marriages, with others who have these experiences suggests that "what are you"/"where are you from" experiences not only influence identity but contribute to mixed-race solidary as well. In the next chapter, we take a closer look at mixed-race parents and their children as we take the study of mixed-race in the US and UK "down a generation."[35]

---

[35]Song 2017: 3.

Chapter 6

"Yes, Girl, Yes. I Want Babies": Mixed-Race Families Generation After Generation

In late 2017 when Prince Harry and Meghan Markle announced their engagement, fashion, guest lists, and potential cost to British tax payers were not the only things on people's minds. As when they were first confirmed to be dating, talk about race instantly followed because Harry is White and Meghan is Black/White mixed-race. For example, it was quickly reported that some hailed the engagement as "a beacon of progress for the UK and its royal family,"[1] even though research in the mixed-race melting pot of Brazil[2] has long demonstrated that White men marrying mixed-race/light skinned women of African descent is perfectly compatible with the continued functioning of White supremacist oppression. Additionally, the differential conceptualisation of race in the US and UK was on full display as readers of *The Guardian* declared "I love the idea of a mixed-race princess"[3] whilst in the US people on Twitter reacted to the idea of a #BlackPrincess.

Buckingham Palace's 2018 announcement that the Duke and Duchess of Sussex were expecting their first child highlights an emerging turn in Critical Mixed Race Studies (CMRS): focus on mixed-race people as adults who form relationships and families of their own. In traditional CMRS scholarship, mixed-race people are defined as the offspring of interracial couples. Even when interviewees or respondents are adults, research questions on their families situates them as the children in their family of origin. Nevertheless, six of Sims' interviewees were already parents themselves at the time of the study; and of the 24 interviewees who did not yet have children, all but one responded in various degrees of affirmative to the question of desire for future children. From a lukewarm "I'm coming around more to the idea" (Lisa, 40, UK, Black/White) to a nonchalant "of

---

[1]Gil 2017.
[2]Hordge-Freeman 2015; Osuji 2019; Telles 2006.
[3]*The Guardian*, 27/11/2017.

Mixed-Race in the US and UK: Comparing the Past, Present, and Future, 79–91
Copyright © 2020 by Jennifer Patrice Sims and Chinelo L. Njaka
Published under exclusive licence
doi:10.1108/978-1-78769-553-520191007

course" (John, 25, US, Black/white) to an excited "Yes, girl, yes. I want babies" (Heather, 25, US, Asian/Black), mixed-race adults have and/or are planning to have children of their own.

Whilst a literature on mixed-race people dating, especially online dating, and forming romantic relationships has recently emerged,[4] Bratter's (2007) statistical analysis in the US and Song's (2017) qualitative interviews in the UK are the first major sociological works to take the study of mixed-race people "down a generation" to examined mixed-race people as parents.[5] This chapter builds on these path-breaking research studies to provide qualitative insight into US mixed-race people's thoughts about children and experiences as parents. The parents and almost half of the non-parents (11, disproportionately of black heritage[6]) in Sims' sample revealed having thought in detail about their partners and their uncertainty regarding what race their children would "be." Their concerns over their future children's race simultaneously focussed on appearance and culture. Discussing both of these themes, this chapter compares and contrasts with Song's findings from her interviews with mixed-race parents in the UK. Parents' accounts from both nations reveal what it is like to experience both the non-parents' hypothesised scenarios as well as additional racialised parenting issues that non-parents apparently had not yet considered.

"Depends on What Their Daddy Is": The Appearance of the Next Generation

Only two of the non-parents who described thinking about race regarding their future children were in relationships at the time of their interview. The other nine were single and very open to dating partners of almost any race. Sara (38, UK, Black/White) illustrates the sentiment by stating, "I don't know what my life partner is going to be, whether Black or White or what." Men also felt this way, exemplified by Mark (49, US, Native American/White) who said that he "never placed any racial requirements on my sweeties."

---

[4]For example, Buggs 2017b, 2019; Currington et al. 2015; Littlejohn 2019; Waring 2013.

[5]Song 2017: 3.

[6]Whilst seven interviewees had non-Black mixed-race backgrounds, only two mentioned pondering race-conscious considerations for their future children; and neither expressed the in-depth concern nor mentioned they had developed partner preferences because of those concerns as did many of the Black mixed-race interviewees. The paucity of data from non-Black mixed-race interviewees on this topic is potentially a result of the data collection process in that because the specific topic of racial concerns for future children was not on the interview guide there is only data from those interviewees who revealed their race-based considerations unprompted. Given that the interviewer was Black, perhaps Black mixed-race interviewees felt more comfortable pre-emptively volunteering their thoughts. As Song's interviewees will demonstrate, when asked directly non-Black mixed-race adults also reveal having pondered considerations regarding the themes of this chapter.

This openness to dating and marrying someone of any race, however, meant that when thinking about their future children, interviewees could not imagine what their children might "look like." This is because whilst there are no genes for "race" the human genome does include genes that code for physical characteristics which are racialised.[7] Vincent (36, UK, Black/White), for example, looks like his Black mother whilst his fraternal twin brother and their sister both look like his White father. Based on the phenotypic diversity in his family, he speculated that "chances are that I could have a white child. Chances are I could have a dark child .... You don't know until you have that child." In other words, as Judy (30, US, Black/White) succinctly put it, the appearance of mixed-race people's children "Depends on what their daddy is."

Pondering different potential future husbands, Judy noted that if she were to have children with a Black man she feels that their genotype would make their phenotype "appear to be Black, period." In this scenario, she says she "probably wouldn't make it a point to reinforce to them, 'Oh, you're mixed.' Or 'You're a quarter White.' Because outwardly it wouldn't matter." John (25, US, Black/White) agrees, saying that if he were to have children with a Black woman their being "a quarter White" would not "contribute to the quality of their lives as far as their identity and blah blah blah." In her statistical analysis of US census data, Bratter found that two-thirds of Black mixed-race people who had Black partners categorised their child as Black.[8] Multivariate analysis revealed that when Black mixed-race women like Judy are partnered with Black men they are 70 per cent less likely to classify their child as mixed-race than a mono-racial Black woman partnered with a non-Black man; this number jumps to 79 per cent less likely for Black mixed-race men like John.[9] As Song noted, qualitative accounts from mixed-race people like Judy and John are necessary to learn the actual thought processes and meaning behind patterns of box ticking.[10]

The majority of the UK mixed-race parents Song interviewed were partnered with Whites, and she explained that "In comparison with the US, Black/White intermarriage is relatively high and increasingly common in Britain."[11] Nevertheless, despite their statistically lower likelihood of partnering with Whites, this scenario was the one that Sims' childless Black/White US interviewees had thought about most in-depth. John, for instance, continued that even though he "never actually dated a White woman," he does think "about that and I think about my kids and I think about their complexion and I think about like what they'll look like." Given that all but two of the 24 childless interviewees had a White parent, it was assumed, to quote Judy, that "having a child with a White guy would most likely mean that my children would look White." This was a concern to some because, as Sydney (39, US, Black/White) explained, "In society, we still are really

---

[7] Kaw 1993; Maclin and Malpass 2001; Sims et al. under review.
[8] Bratter 2007: 836.
[9] Bratter 2007: 838.
[10] Song 2017.
[11] Song 2017: 30.

driven by what you look like. And if you look like a certain thing, people are going to assume that you are that thing." Given that internalisation of reflected appraisals has an influence on racial identity development,[12] Joy (27, US, Black/White) assumed that "If I married a White person, my kids are going to probably identify almost as being White."

Whereas previous research has identified "possible racism" as the factor underlying some mixed-race women's "disinterest or hesitance in regard to White men,"[13] in the present sample having biological children who would potentially look and identify as White is what pushed some Black mixed-race interviewees away from considering Whites as future partners. Though interviewees, like Heather, stressed that "who I fall in love with is who I fall in love with," and emphasised, like Suzie (33, US, Black/White), that they "would love my kids regardless of what color that to they are," they nonetheless expressed preference for non-White, preferably Black, partners, and children. Dean (27, UK, Black/White) for instance said his future partner "hopefully" will be Black because "if I was to have kids with a, like, a White woman and the kids looked really White it would be hard to raise 'em, like, Black."

Judy witnessed this difficulty first hand via her older sister. Her sister, her White mother's daughter with the Creole[14] man she was married to before she married Judy's Black father, "came out looking White" according to Judy. She further explained how her sister's appearance has been "a really big deal for her all her life because people say things in front of her or talk to her or treat her a certain way, assuming that she's White." In the UK, Dave (30, UK, Black/White) discussed how his brother had these experiences into adulthood. In one instance:

> He was working in a bar once and, in the university with a, you know, very high proportion of Black students, and he had this White bartender as well who'd kinda come up to him and go "These fucking Niggers, man, far too many you know." And he didn't realize he wasn't White and that was probably the most poor thing [*sic.*] for my brother, this guy not registering.

In a study that asked mixed-race respondents to recall an instance in which their identity "was brought into focus, causing tension, and making you feel pressure to identify with only one of your racial/ethnic heritages," appearance-based issues topped the list.[15] Research has found that mixed-race people value accurate racial perception,[16] and that misclassification is associated with higher rates on a number of measures of psychological distress.[17]

---

[12]Khanna 2004; Khanna and Johnson 2010; Sims 2016.
[13]Buggs 2019: 1230.
[14]Though "Creole" can apply to a person of any racial designation, Judy's use of the word in juxtaposing her Black father with her phenotypically White sister's father suggests that she was referring to a mixed-race man of White (French) ancestry.
[15]Townsend et al. 2009.
[16]Remedios and Chasteen 2013.
[17]Campbell and Troyer 2007.

As a result of knowing that a person from a Black family who appears White by dominant cultural standards would likely have these types of upsetting experiences, Judy says she "would not be very happy" if she had a White looking child. John's consideration of his future children's appearance (coupled with the claim that he is "not attracted to White women anyway") led him to cautiously hypothesise that "there's no way I would think, at least at this point, listen to me predicting the future, but would have kids with a White woman. I don't think I would."

Although genotype's influence on phenotype is not infallibly directed, the non-parents' speculation about the results that partnering with White partners might have for their children's appearance were quite astute. Based on the pictures of relatives that people showed during their interviews, Joy's nephews and Sydney's son, who all have White fathers, were phenotypically White. Among Song's UK sample, many of the first generation Black/White mixed-race people who had children with a White partner had second-generation mixed-race children who were seen as racially ambiguous not White by others. Second-generation Black/White interviewees with White partners, however, did have third-generation Black/White mixed-race children who were phenotypically White. The fact that slave descent, "mono-racial" US Blacks, like Joy's and Sydney's Black parents, have a significant proportion of White ancestors due to the systematic rape of enslaved Black women by White men[18] could explain why, in the US, "second" generation Black/White mixed-race people phenotypically resemble their third-generation UK counterparts.

As Sydney searched for a picture to show, she explained that "it is kind of an interesting experience for me, to have a child who I consider mixed-race but the rest of the world doesn't." Most of the mixed-race UK parents Song studied also insisted that their children were mixed-race and "refused to let physical appearance determine how" they identified them.[19] Like Sydney, though, some parents in the UK nonetheless found it an "interesting" experience to have a child who appeared White. One Asian/White woman interviewed by Song, for example, admitted that she was "completely stunned," and "a bit disappointed," that both of her children "came out blonde with blue eyes" because that "wasn't what I was expecting at all."[20]

Whereas non-parents in the US had predicted the possibility of having phenotypically White children, one aspect of physical appearance they did not touch on was family resemblances. Sydney revealed, however, that she gets mistaken for her son's nanny; and in the UK, Song's interviewees additionally told of some people's "almost visceral alarm and disgust" in response to seeing parents and children who did not resemble each other, as in the case of a Black/White man kissing his elderly White mum in public.[21] Whilst looking at a picture of her son, Sydney recalled that "there was a picture of me when I'm about three. [My son and I] have

---

[18]Gates 2014.
[19]Song 2017: 44.
[20]Song 2017: 139.
[21]Song 2017: 100.

the exact same face." She exasperates that people "can't get past color" to see the physical features that she and her son do share. Hearing "'He looks just like your husband. He doesn't look like you at all'" frustrates her because:

> Don't get me wrong, he does look like my husband. And that's a good thing. I want him to. I'm like come on. And he is his son and he's a boy. And I get the whole gestalt is sort of my husband. But he actually looks a lot like me. And sometimes I'm like "Hey!"

Though the non-parents in the sample did not mention thinking about parent–child resemblance, this theme is found in the literature on donor-assisted reproduction. Among heterosexually married women in the US, for example, research finds that resemblance to one's husband is an important criteria when selecting a sperm donor.[22] Likewise, White lesbians in both nations report consciously selecting sperm donors who "match" the non-birth mother (or both partners) on hair, eye, and skin colour; and gay male couples have been found to select egg donors whose "physical, cultural, and vocational characteristics are similar to themselves."[23] Sydney's sentiments echo these parents' desires for a child who will be perceived by generalised others as "looking like" them.

"That Could've Been My Son": From Family Resemblances to Institutional Racism

In addition to not foreseeing issues regarding family (non)resemblance, Black mixed-race non-parents also failed to articulate any premeditation on the specific issues that the phenotypically Black children they desired would face in White supremacist societies. Two such topics, hair and violence, were discussed by Tia (37, US, Black/Native American/White) and Aaliyah (25, US, Black/White) whose children with Black men were all phenotypically Black.

Regarding hair, value-laden perceptions of hair are especially acute for Black and Black mixed-race people given that hair is constructed as "communicating" information such as the person's personal, social, and political ideologies.[24] Starting from the mid-twentieth century, Afrocentric hairstyles have come to symbolise racial authenticity for Blacks[25]; and although hairstyles are often chosen for non-ideological reasons such as fashion or ease of care, within the current symbolic framework straightened versus curly/natural hairstyles are, nonetheless, often reductively interpreted as evidence that a person accepts Eurocentric versus Afrocentric standards, respectively.[26]

---

[22]Hanson 2001; Szkupinski 2007.
[23]Mitchell and Green 2007: 87; Nordqvist 2010: 1138; Ryan et al. 2010.
[24]Gilchrist and Jackson 2012; Tate 2007.
[25]Tate 2007.
[26]Gilchrist and Jackson 2012.

The negative evaluation of natural textured African hairstyles continues today in both the US and UK in politics, business, education, and other areas. Online survey experiments that vary a Black woman's hairstyle found that "employment candidates with Afrocentric hairstyles were rated as less professional and less likely to succeed in Corporate America than employment candidates with Eurocentric hairstyles."[27] Experiments varying a hypothetical Black woman political candidate's hairstyle resulted in voters reporting different perceptions of her assumed political ideology (e.g. conservative or liberal), traits (e.g. level of experience and work ethic), and behaviours (e.g. actions she might take on key issues).[28] Educational institutions in both nations also deprive racial minority students of equal educational opportunities by policing and punishing them for wearing non-Eurocentric hairstyles, which are deemed "faddish," "extreme," or "distracting."[29] Race scholars argue that Black hair in particular is a "site of social control" and that schools' hairstyle policing maintains and perpetuates White supremacy by using "race-neutral or 'colourblind'" polices to "re(produce) and normalize surface-level manifestations of anti-Blackness."[30]

In her book *Don't Touch My Hair* (2019), Emma Dabiri reveals that as a Black/White mixed-race woman growing up in Ireland her hair was a constant source of deep shame.[31] Sims' Black mixed-race interviewees likewise discussed their own painful experiences in relation to Eurocentric, colonial ideologies that devalue Black hair; however, none of the childless interviewees mentioned thinking about their future children's potential hair textures or how that might influence their social experiences. Tia, a mother to three girls and two boys, however, did discuss her daughters' hair, explaining how she helps her girls respond to society's devaluation of it. For example, she recalled an incident when another child explicitly compared her long and loosely curled hair to her oldest daughter's short, coarse, and tightly curled hair:

> We actually just had a girl at the Boys and Girls Club say to my oldest daughter "Oh, that's your mom? Oh, she does have a lot of hair. What happened to you?" Which my daughter was like, "Ugh, what do you mean?"

The tones of voice that Tia used to recount the girl's comments – incredulous ("Oh, that's your mom?"), admiring ("Oh, does she have a lot of hair"), then degrading ("What happened to you?") – suggests that this girl was insinuating that Tia's daughter's hair was less attractive than Tia's. Though neither the non-parents in Sims' US sample nor the parents in Song's UK sample discussed hair, Tia's story offers a reminder that one of the subtle forms of colourblind racism

---

27Opie and Phillips 2015: 5.
28Lemi and Brown 2019.
29Nittle 2017.
30Joseph-Salisbury and Connelly 2018: 219.
31Dabiri 2019.

that multigenerationally Black mixed-race children may face is the continued stigmatisation of Afrocentric aesthetics. Though Tia only related the one story about her oldest daughter, she ended by emphasising that all three girls "are having those experiences. The only thing that really, I guess, identifies it for them is the texture of their hair." As a mother she is "watching that change and seeing the differences there" so that she can continue to affirm her daughters' appearance and identities in the face of anti-Blackness.

Another topic that non-parents did not discuss was that of having a pheno-typically Black child in societies that have a common history and contemporary tradition of police and vigilante violence against Black and Black mixed-race people. Whilst this impacts people in the UK (e.g. Mark Duggan), the issue is especially acute in the US given the juxtaposition of police officers' ability to arrest murderous White men alive (e.g. the Aurora movie theatre shooter) with their demonstrated inability to refrain from shooting Black children within mere seconds of laying eyes on them (e.g. Tamir Rice).

The issues of violence against Blacks is also an issue of colourism.[32] Monk's work, for instance, has found that skin colour has significant effects on multiple stratification outcomes including health disparities and disparities within the criminal justice system.[33] In an article soberingly titled "Looking Deathworthy," other researchers compared the sentences of Black men who were convicted of murder and found that, all else equal, about twice as many darker skinned Black men with Afrocentric features had received the death penalty compared to lighter skinned Black men with Eurocentric features.[34] In short, there are dangers to being perceived as Black within White supremacist societies.

Physically, "even though he's a quarter White" Aaliyah's son with a Black man "is darker skinned than both me and my fiancé." Despite her son being very young at the time of her interview, Aaliyah mentioned having already thought about this issue. She remembered that when George Zimmerman killed Trayvon Martin she was:

> so affected by that just because I was like, it's happened you know throughout history, but this is the case where I'd actually had a son and this is the first time [as a mother] I'm hearing of this Black teenager shot for no reason. And it was just like the fact that his race made him suspicious and made this other person want to follow and then kill him and that could've been my son.

---

[32]See Russell et al. (1992); Herring (2004: 3, 18) defines colorism as "the discriminatory treatment of individuals falling within the same 'racial' group basis of skin color" as well as "other phenotypic features such as eye color, hair texture, broadness of nose, and fullness of lips."

[33]Monk 2014, 2015, 2019.

[34]Eberhardt et al. 2006.

For this reason, despite recognising that her son is mixed-race, she emphasises a Black identity more than a mixed-race identity because:

> I really want to be careful and cognizant that he understands his Black identity and knows what it means to be like a Black male in the US .... I want him to be very aware that he is Black and he is growing up in the United States and [it] has this history of racism that still occurs today.

In sum, Tia and Aaliyah talked candidly about the substantial racial animus that their phenotypically Black children either have faced or potentially could face. Because their children appeared racially ambiguous or White, Song's mixed-race interviewees' main considerations regarding their children and racism were of potential ridicule, not systemic social devaluation or death. Thus, as with what race their child will "be," whether a mixed-race parent's socialisation of their children focusses on micro-aggressions or deadly aggressions depends on "what they come out looking like."

"I Wouldn't Want What's Valuable to Me to Get Lost": The Culture of the Next Generation

In addition to physical appearance, the childless interviewees in Sims' sample also thought about their future children's culture and ethnicity. Like Frost (28, US, Black/Latino), about a third reported that whilst they may "let them know their roots" they "would encourage them not to let that influence their behavior" or "let it influence their self-perception." In contrast, another third felt like Sally (19, US, Asian/White) who said "I want to teach them a little bit of everything." The final group of childless interviewees (all Black mixed-race), like Fleur (34, UK, Black/White) desired to pass on to their children, not "everything," but "the dark side of my cultural heritage."

In expressing their desire to pass on culture to their children, the childless mixed-race adults planned to do so mainly via trips to heritage countries but also via consumption of toys, books, movies, food, and other cultural items from or that feature their future children's heritage(s). Both US and UK parents report engaging in these exact activities. For example, Tia takes her children to the annual PowWow held in their city. In the UK, Mary (41, UK Asian/White) says she "grew up going backwards and forward to Italy;" and now that she is married with children of her own, she has "continued that as our own family." She also cooks Iranian food "when I can remember how," and as her husband George (41, UK, Asian/Black) is from a mixed-race Jamaican family, she cooks West Indian food as well. Sara, the only person to mention considering adoption, planned to socialise her future adopted child in the same manner as those with or planning to have biological children.

Non-parents also recognised that their (future) partner's culture may be imparted to their children as well; and this realisation was cause for concern for some Black mixed-race people. Annette's (31, US, Black/White) fiancé is Latino, and though he knows his family are descended from Spanish, Basque, and Apache, according to Annette he identifies with the dominant, heavily Mexican, pan-Latino culture of southern California. This bothers her because "I want our [future] kids to grow up kind of recognizing their different heritages. The thing that I'm concerned about is that Hispanic ends up kind of engulfing everything else." Heather expressed a generalised version of Annette's sentiment by simply hoping that "where I come from is important to [my future children]."

This hope influenced a few single Black mixed-race US interviewees to have partner preferences. Joy, in addition to speculating that her children with a White man would potently be phenotypically White, further explained her rejection of White men as potential partners as due to the cultural experiences she wants her children to have:

> My experience has really only been in the Black community. And it's important to me that my kids have that identity. And I don't feel like my kids would if I was with a White man. No matter how many Black friends he may have or whatever.

Song, too, discussed a Black/White UK interviewee who expressed an "aversion to dating White men because of her wish to retain the 'Black line.' "[35] In the US, though, Joy continued on to explain that it was not any Black heritage she wanted to pass on, but specifically her African American ethnicity. She recalled a time when she seriously dated an Eritrean man:

> His family is still very, very much like hold onto all their traditions and everything. And for me it was like, even though I thought, oh-. ... would my kids more strongly identify with their culture and their history? And then what I feel is the strength of Black American history, would that get lost? ... his culture may seem more dominant, um like I wouldn't want what's valuable to me to get lost in there.

Concerns with one's culture being "lost" were evident in Song's UK sample too. Some of her Asian/White interviewees who had White partners expressed sadness about what she termed "ethnic dilution," that is, the "cultural loss of a minority heritage" in subsequent generations.[36] Though this theme was quite prevalent among Asian/White mixed-race parents in Song's sample, none of Sims' Asian/White non-parents discussed it. Mark, the only Native American/White interviewee, on the other hand, did mention an awareness of ethnic dilution. The sole interviewee to respond that he definitely did not want children, he none-theless shared that if he were to have children unless their mother were a Native American woman from his exact tribe (Rosebud Sioux), then his children would

---

[35]Song 2017: 133.
[36]Song 2017: 137.

be ineligible to be the members of the tribe due to not meeting the blood quantum requirements. Unlike others in Sims' and Song's studies, however, Mark did not seem concerned with this.

The Black/White interviewees in Sims' sample who were most concerned with the possibility of ethnic dilution all viewed themselves as having one heritage, Black (US) American. For example, when asked what he might teach his future children about their White side of the family, John responded with annoyance boarding on offense: "What do I have to educate them about that? And the truth is nothing. 'Cause I don't. My mom's fucking White. That's all I got." These interviewees all mono-racially identified as Black and considered Black American to be their only cultural heritage. With respect to the culture that their future children would receive from them, therefore, Black American culture was of the utmost importance to pass on because, despite one of their parents being White, Black was considered the entirety of their culture. Their preference for Black partners, then, stems from a very difference place than the colourblind sexual racism that research has revealed underlays other populations' contemporary race-based "personal preferences."[37] Rather than excluding members of certain races as potential partners in accordance with hegemonic White supremacist devaluation of those groups, these interviewees' preferences flow from a desire to preserve minority culture in spite of dominant messages that negate its value.

Despite the focus on Black *American* identity, though, US interviewees did not mention imparting a national identity to their children. That is, none of the US interviewees planned to impart (childless) or were imparting (parents) a racially "neutral"[38] "American" identity. In the UK, by contrast, although the vast majority of Song's mixed-race parents were raising their children with a "cosmopolitan" approach which celebrated being mixed-race as part of an increasingly diverse Britain, about a third of the sample were socialising their children to identities centred on understandings of Britishness. This could include being mostly White British or being British but with other symbolic ethnicities[39] and echoes the finding in Chapter 3 that racial identities are expressed in tandem with national identities in the UK.

Nevertheless, whether "racial" or "national," parental socialisation is not destiny and it does not always mean that a mixed-race person's child will ultimately adopt the cultural orientation their parents attempted to impart. Though they had considered the possibility of one parent's culture being more dominant in their children's lives, the strength of peer influence was a factor that was not considered by non-parents. Recall Annette's fears that her fiancé's southern California pan-Latino culture could dominate their future children's identity. Carmen (31, US, Asian/Black/Latino/White), her boyfriend (also mixed-race), and their four kids also live in southern California; and although she and her boyfriend identify as Black and are socialising their children to a Black identity, she reports

---

[37]Robinson 2016.
[38]Devos and Banaji 2005.
[39]Song 2017.

that their son would prefer to identify as Latino like the majority of his peers. She describes how:

> sometimes he talks with, like, an accent. One day he told me he wished his name was, like, José. And I was like, "Honey, you do know that you're Black. You do know that we're not bilingual. You are mixed, yes, but we are not full Hispanic." And he's like "I know."

As Annette predicted, Latino "ended up engulfing everything else" for Carmen's son. The influence came from peers and his community, however, not either of his parents. Non-parents, then, were correct that their future children's cultural orientation will depend upon what exposure and involvement they receive. However, in only thinking about their and their (future) partner's cultures, they underestimated the power of peers and the broader social environment to influence what their future children grow to "be."

Conclusion

Mixed-Race adults and their children may not herald the end of racism but they do highlight the fact that the traditional understanding of mixed-race has been that they are the offspring of two "mono" racial parents. Sims' and Song's interview studies with mixed-race parents and aspiring parents reveal the processes of mixed-race "a generation down" in the US and UK. Many mixed-race adults think long and hard about race and their present and future children. Single adults' openness to dating and marrying someone of any race, for instance, makes it difficult to imagine what second- and third-generation mixed-race children might "look like" and "be" with regard to race. Although there is no race gene, because genotype influences phenotype and because there are symbolic associations of certain physical features with certain races, mixed-race adults acknowledge that their children's appearance will "depend on what their daddy is." Despite Black/White intermarriage being more prominent in the UK than the US, partnering with Whites and potentially having children who others may racialise as White was the potential scenario that most concerned Black/White US interviewees and pushed a few to the decision to only date people of colour. Others' inability to "get past colour" and see that mixed-race parents and children resemble each other, also concerned some mixed-race parents in both nations.

Lack of others recognising family resemblance was the least of some mixed-race parents' worries though. In both the US and UK, Black mixed-race parents face the task of helping their multigenerationally Black mixed-race children navigate the subtle colourblind racism that is the continued stigmatisation of Afrocentric hair and the overt violent racism that is systemic police and vigilantly murder of Black people. Given that the main considerations of parents of White appearing children were of potential ridicule, the continued influence of colourism on mixed-race experiences generation after generation is clear.

Parents and aspiring parents also recognised the role of culture and racial socialisation in what their children would "be." Most expressed a desire to pass on their racial heritage(s) to their children, and UK interviewees additionally discussed cultural transmission of national identities as well. Nevertheless, recognising that parental socialisation does not automatically mean that a mixed-race person's child will adopt the cultural orientation their parents attempt to impart, some interviewees in both nations were troubled by the potential for cultural loss of their minority heritage in future generations, a phenomenon Song terms "ethnic dilution."

In sum, despite some differences, the theme throughout interviewees' discussions in both nations is that many mixed-race people have a racial consciousness and are keenly aware of the interplay between biology and society in constructing race. When thinking about the generation after next, that is, about their children's future partners and their grandchildren, both US and UK parents expressed a cosmopolitan ethos and an openness to whoever made their children happy. Referring to her son, Aaliyah asserted that she "would not care if he met a White woman and that's who he fell in love with. That's fine." In the UK, this openness also extended to the gender of their children's future partners with many of the parents Song interviewed "saying they wouldn't care if their child partnered with someone of the same sex."[40] Since the majority of CMRS research has focussed on heterosexual populations, the next chapter offers a look into Lesbian, Gay, Bisexual, Transgender, Queer, Intersex, and Asexual mixed-race people's experiences.

---

[40]Song: 2017: 127.

Chapter 7

Queering Critical Mixed Race Studies

As discussed in the Introduction, academic attention to mixed-race populations increased in the 1980s and throughout the 1990s and early 2000s. In line with the general homophobia and heteronormativity of that time period, Critical Mixed Race Studies (CMRS) often and uncritically centred heterosexuality. Whilst the US and the UK are slowly becoming more accepting of sexual diversity,[1] so too has CMRS begun to pay more attention to mixed-race people who identity as Lesbian, Gay, Bisexual, Transgender, Queer, Intersex, and Asexual (LGBTQIA). This chapter decentres traditional heteronormativity to focus on their experiences. After first discussing the importance of attention to sexuality vis-à-vis race in general, the limited literature on queer mixed-race populations is reviewed. The second half of the chapter then presents preliminary findings on queer Black mixed-race men and women from an in-progress study of mixed-race people who identity as LGBTQIA.

The Intersection of Race and Sexuality

In a recent book simply titled *Race and Sexuality*, Vidal-Ortiz et al. (2018) remind social scientists that the titular social systems operate synchronously not separately or additively.[2] Of the structural level of analysis, they explain how "sexuality is often erased or invisible in how most people conceptualize racial formations," pointing out that White and male dominated research on racial formation projects have traditionally overlooked the centrality of sexuality.[3] Regarding US slavery, for example, White men's systematic rape of enslaved Black women has typically

---

[1]Pew Research Center, quoted in Drake 2013; British Social Attitudes Survey, quoted in Clements 2017.
[2]We label their points a reminder because whilst they list notable social science research at the intersectionality of race and sexually (15) they point out that scholars within the humanities have "more actively produced scholarship that views race, gender, and sexuality in inherently interconnected ways" than social scientists (16).
[3]Vidal-Ortiz et al. 2018: 27.

Mixed-Race in the US and UK: Comparing the Past, Present, and Future, 93–101
Copyright © 2020 by Jennifer Patrice Sims and Chinelo L. Njaka
Published under exclusive licence
doi:10.1108/978-1-78769-553-520191008

been under-acknowledged in analyses of slavery's role in constructing ideas of race except in the marginalised work of women of colour scholars, activists, and artists.[4] At the micro-level, they remind scholars that ways of "doing race" occur through sexuality and ways of "doing gender" are in fact raced.[5] From analyses of several historical and contemporary examples, the authors demonstrate how the "discursive and structural elements of society around race and sexuality produce certain raced sexual readings of particular bodies" which then have "concrete material and social lived consequences."[6]

With regard to the intersection of race and sexuality for mixed-race people, few theorists have specifically attempted to "queer multiracial theory" or to incorporate mixedness into queer theory.[7] In addition, few empirical studies of mixed-race populations have included more than token representation of LGBTQIA mixed-race people or have attempted to theoretically tease out queer experiences during their analysis of predominantly heterosexual samples. Early writing that attempted to do this began with mixed-race queer women, noting that mixed-race women's "lived experience of understanding racial identity as complex" may "transfer over" to viewing sexual orientation and sexual identity as "flexible" and "mutable" thus allowing them to "be more open to exploring sexual orientation."[8] Speaking of her own experiences, Thomson (2000b) illuminated the similarities in racial and sexual identity development when she recalled that:

> As I had years earlier agonized between the choice of seeing myself as Chinese or White, I now agonized between the choice of lesbian or straight. I knew that neither choice represented my feelings, yet I could not comprehend another option.[9]

Thus, whilst structures of race and sexuality are not identically constructed or perfectly analogous, their shared assumptions of mutually exclusive categorisation are experienced as constraining and othering to those who occupy multiple categories. At the same time, though, the systems can work in tandem. Both Thompson (Chinese/White) and mixed-race Chicana feminist Cherrie Moraga (Chicana/White) write about how embracing their bisexuality and lesbianism, respectively, "reawakened" a "profound connection" to their racial minority heritage.[10] In other words, rather than being experienced as discrete and different identities, race and sexuality come "together in a complimentary fashion" for queer mixed-race women.[11] King's (2011) interviews with six mixed-race bi/pansexual women identifies college as a key context for exploring, practicing

---

[4]Vidal-Ortiz et al. 2018: 31–32.

[5]Vidal-Ortiz et al. 2018: 32, 38.

[6]Vidal-Ortiz et al. 2018: 45, 59.

[7]See Thompson 2000a for a review.

[8]Thompson 2000b:174; Root 1990: 185.

[9]Thompson 2000b: 174.

[10]Moraga 2015[1979]: 28; Thompson 2000b: 175.

[11]Thompson 2000b: 174.

using labels, participating in cultural activities, and learning to negotiate one's race and sexuality.[12]

Beyond individual identity development, King's work also examined experiences being uniquely marginalised in social settings at the intersections of systems of oppression. She found that many of her interviewees described "experiences of struggling to find places to belong, whether with new friends or within clubs and organizations in the college setting, as they thought about and processed their racial and sexual identities."[13] From interviews with nine bisexual Asian/White biracial women, "bi bi girls" as she calls them, Thompson explains that because social communities and organisations typically form around singular identities, bi bi girls repeatedly have the "painful experience" of having one of their identities obscured, denied, and/or rejected.[14] In fact, all nine of her interviewees expressed "discontent with the 'established' gay and lesbian community for being monolithically White" as well as biphobic.[15] There was also the parallel spectre of isolation within or homophobic rejection from communities of colour. Nevertheless, Thompson's bisexual Asian/White interviewees felt "more affinity and connection to racial/ethnic based communities or organizations" because they felt "more included within racial/ethnic organizations in which they 'look like everyone else' than in gay and lesbian organizations, where they share a more covert identity yet stand out physically."[16]

Physical appearance is also a prominent factor in the experiences of Black/White mixed-race people. Waring (2013) finds that others code Black/White mixed-race people as "exotic" but that it is experienced differently by gender and sexual orientation.[17] After discussing how being considered "exotic" is associated with different patterns of sexual encounters for heterosexual men and women, she explains that no gay interviewees "explicitly referenced sexual encounters with respect to being 'exoticized.'"[18] Whilst a gay man interviewee reported being considered "gorgeous"[19] just like his heterosexual counterparts, it did not facilitate sexual encounters for him as it did for heterosexuals. In fact, in some cases, his physical appearance was a hindrance. Waring explained that "non-White men do not view him as exotic and in fact his light skin complexion is 'disruptive' in such communities."[20] Being considered "*too* light-skinned" by

---

[12]King 2011.
[13]King 2011: 448.
[14]Thompson 2000b: 176.
[15]Thompson 2000b: 176; Thompson 2012: 418.
[16]Thompson 2012: 421–422.
[17]Waring 2013. Whilst this characterisation was applied to all, Waring found that interviewees who were racially ambiguous (defined as being frequently misperceived racially) often took it as a compliment, a phenomenon she explained as due to their internalised colourblind ideology.
[18]Waring 2013: 312.
[19]See Sims 2012 on the Biracial Beauty Stereotype that mixed-race people are always extraordinarily attractive.
[20]Anzaldúa 1987; Waring 2013: 306.

Black men, for example, had influenced his pattern of dating mostly White men as they were "intrigued" by his "exotic" appearance.[21] In short, though the particular manifestations may be different, as Buggs (2017) explains "sexual racism and racial fetishism more broadly are integral parts of the dating experiences" for mixed-race people.[22]

Preliminary Findings from Interviews with LGBTQIA Mixed-Race People

As described in detail in the Methodological Appendix, Sims' current research project is examining LGBTQIA mixed-race people's experiences with others' perception of their race, gender, and sexuality. It also examines the dynamics and importance of their interpersonal relationships with peers for identity development. As of this writing, 16 people, aged 15–50, had been interviewed. Black/White ($N = 6$) and Asian/white ($N = 5$) comprised the largest heritage groups and the majority identified as gay, lesbian, and/or queer. With seven cis women, one trans woman, seven cis men, and one non-binary person, the gender and sexual diversity of these first interviewees is already significantly more pronounced than most CMRS research samples.

Building on Sims and Joseph-Salisbury's (2019) finding that "the differential dynamics of gender within the heterosexual matrix diverges [heterosexual Black mixed-race men's and women's] experiences with peers in identity-salient ways,"[23] the remainder of this chapter presents preliminary findings from the first US Black mixed-race LGBTQIA interviewees regarding their identity development vis-à-vis the Black community. It illuminates how white supremacist constructions of Black masculinity and heteronormative constructions of femininity influence queer interviewees' experiences with peers as well, albeit with less clear cut influence on racial identity.

"That's Not Me": Black Mixed-Race Gay Men

Research on predominantly heterosexual samples of Black mixed-race men has found inclusion in Black men's peer groups, especially during adolescence, to be both normative and an important mechanism by which Black racial identity develops.[24] The Black mixed-race gay men in this sample, however, did *not* report close friendships with Black men. Instead, interviewees reported that their friendship groups were all women or were diverse. Charles (34, US, Black/Native American/Mexican/White, gay man) recalled that in high school his "clique" was "me and the three other overachieving Black girls who are all engineers now." Andrew (27, US, Black/White, gay man), who describes himself as "very feminine,"

---

[21]Waring 2013: 306, emphasis in original.
[22]Buggs 2017a: 4.
[23]Sims and Joseph-Salisbury 2019: 62.
[24]Joseph-Salisbury 2018; Sims and Joseph-Salisbury 2019.

was also friends with girls in high school. He says that since there was lots of homophobic bullying at his first high school he chose to befriend the popular "upper middle class White female students" for protection. He explained that he would "commodify my gayness to them and be sort of an entertaining personality" because by "being associated with them, I was exempted from a lot of people's bullshit."[25]

Another Black mixed-race gay man discussed being a member of a diverse "outcast" group. Anthony (34, US, Black/White, gay man) explained that he "just sort of fell in with the outcasts" who were Goth kids, gay kids and "weird" kids in his middle and high school. He explained how, despite their differences, he and his friends "kind of connected at that level" because "We were all kind of outcasts in our own different ways." Like Thompson's bi bi girls, then, Black mixed-race gay men likewise appear to have "constructed communities based upon a diversity of individuals across race, sexuality, gender, and person interests."[26]

All of the Black mixed-race gay men interviewed so far report identifying primarily as mixed-race versus Black. This is in contrast to the typical Black centred racial identity that studies of mainly heterosexual Black mixed-race men have reported. Joseph-Salisbury's work explains how race, gender, and heterosexuality intersect for their identity development.[27] Since gender is constructed within the heterosexual matrix to mean being attractive and attracted to the "opposite" gender,[28] Black mixed-race men are able to successfully "do gender,"[29] that is perform masculinity, when they are desired by women due to colourism and when this desirability facilitates their successful enactment of masculine gendered behaviours such as "predatory rituals of getting girls."[30] Their Black centred racial identity thus develops in part due to their acceptance from and popularity within peer groups of Black men.

The one Black mixed-race gay man interviewed by Joseph-Salisbury, on the other hand, discussed how "his sexuality rendered him outside of the Black man same."[31] Likewise, the Black mixed-race gay men interviewed so far for this study feel that their divergence from heteronormative Black masculine standards lead to rejection from Black peers, not acceptance. Anthony, for example, described his young self as "nerdy" and "very stereotypical" gay, and he recalled "being called out for not being Black enough essentially." Patricia Hill Collins (2004) explains in *Black Sexual Politics* that racist oppression has traditionally denied Black men the ability to achieve the traditional characteristics associated with hegemonic masculinity (e.g. wealth, property, and patriarchal power), therefore

---

[25]Despite the efficacy of his strategy, Andrew "hated doing that" and soon left the school.
[26]Thompson 2012: 423.
[27]Joseph-Salisbury 2018; Sims and Joseph-Salisbury 2019.
[28]Butler 1990.
[29]Butler 1990; Garfinkel 1967; West and Fensermaker 1995; West and Zimmerman 1987.
[30]Pascoe 2011; Sims and Joseph-Salisbury 2019.
[31]Joseph-Salisbury 2018: 164.

Black masculinity has been constructed with reference to "other markers mas-culinity, namely, sexual prowess and brute strength."[32] The "sexual prowess," however, is more specifically hyper-heterosexuality. In short, Black masculinity became defined in terms of sexual domination over women.[33] Black mixed-race gay men who are feminine and/or friends with, not the sexual partners of, women, therefore, are constructed not just outside of masculinity in general but outside of Black masculinity in particular.

Charles expressed these processes clearly when talking about his heterosexual brother. Stating that he feels that the "Black community" does not accept "very feminine" Black mixed-race gay men such as himself, he illustrated by contrasting his mixed-race identity with his brother's Black identity:

> My brother, who is much much lighter skinned than I am, very much identifies as Black ... As he became more of this gross heterosexual pig, the Black community really embraced him. And I was like, "Oh, that's not me." And they were like, "Get the fuck out."

Several factors are of key importance in this account. First, Charles notes that his brother is lighter skinned than him yet is accepted as Black due to his success-ful performance of hegemonic Black masculinity. This underscores that whilst race is socially constructed based in part on physical characteristics, "doing" race via culturally specific associated behaviours is also a critical element.

Second, perceived rejection from the Black community appears to push Black mixed-race gay men away from identification as Black. Given that White and other identities are largely unavailable (due to cultural norms of hypodescent as discussed in previous chapters) and/or undesired (due to negative experiences of prejudice from Whites), for most Black/White mixed-race people a push away from Blackness results in strong mixed-race identity.[34] More to the point, this appears to occur *despite acceptance* from other Blacks within the community. Recall that Charles' high school friendship group consisted of him and three Black women. His characterisation of rejection from the "Black community," despite being best friends with three women from the community, suggests that the "Black community" to which he is referring is actually a specific subset of Blacks. Since the Black women Charles was friends with were more specifically women who entered into a traditionally masculine occupational field (Engineer-ing), perhaps the "Black community" whose acceptance or rejection is influen-tial to Black mixed-race men's identity development is the subset of Blacks who accept the dominant ideas about Black gender and sexuality. In this way, White supremacist constructions, though articulated through Black people, continue to define Black masculinity by deeming alternative forms of expression that do not

---

[32]Collins 2004: 58.
[33]Collins 2004.
[34]Khanna 2011; Rockquemore and Laszloffy 2005.

adhere to traditional controlling images of Blackness as "not being Black enough essentially."

"They would pull my hair": *Black Mixed-Race Queer Women*

In contrast to the emerging picture for gay men, Black mixed-race heterosexual women's *successful* accomplishment of hegemonic femininity is what has been associated with rejection from same gender Black peers and the development of a mixed-race centred identity. Khanna (2011), for instance, found that 61.3 per cent of Black/White mixed-race women responded that they had experienced "hostility and negative treatment from Black people."[35] This phenomenon is echoed in other studies of mainly heterosexual Black mixed-race women[36] and in Black literature.[37]

Rockquemore and Laszloffy (2005) explain that within a heteronormative White patriarchal society women are positioned against each other as competitors for men's attention (and its accompanying social and material resources); thus, Black mixed-race women's frequent possession of more highly valued feminine traits such as lighter skin or straighter hair can be a source of conflict when Black women recognise and justifiably resent being devalued in society vis-à-vis Black mixed-race women.[38] As Fanon explained, oppressed groups will first direct their frustration at injustice against their own people and/or differently oppressed people.[39]

Two of the queer women in this sample described experiencing the same type of appearance-based hostility from Black girls at their school as Black mixed-race heterosexual women in previous studies. Shawn (27, US, Black/Creole, asexual woman), for example, is an asexual woman with a very feminine self-presentation, and she recalled that "a lot of the Black kids, really the girls, were the only ones who would go out of their way to be mean and harass me." Like many straight women, the tone of the harassment was gendered and raced, focussing on her physical traits, mainly her hair type and light skin colour. She recalled that "they would pull my hair. I had this one girl who would constantly bully me just like they would call me names like half breed or White girl."

Another interviewee, Sarah (27, US, multiracial Dominican, lesbian woman) also reported experiencing bullying in her youth. Like Shawn, she felt that it had more to do with racialised gender hierarchies than sexual orientation. Sarah explained how her mother interpreted the bullying as due to other girls' "jealousy" at Sarah's appearance – "beautiful hair" and a face that was not "common" like theirs. Ethnographic research has shown that Dominicans' notions of "beautiful hair" are racialised and that Eurocentric texture and styles such as straight

---

[35]Khanna 2011: 72.
[36]Rockquemore and Laszloffy 2005; Sims 2014.
[37]Taylor 1981.
[38]Rockquemore and Laszloffy 2005: 131–132.
[39]Fanon 1961.

hair are considered more beautiful than Afrocentric texture and styles.[40] Like the names that Shawn was called, others' purported perception of Sarah exists at the intersection of race and gender hierarchies.

The fact that neither Shawn nor Sarah expressed interest in straight Black men and made no actions to attract or date them, yet both were still bullied by Black women peers, suggests that experiences within the heterosexual matrix are, at their core, not about women's sexuality but are about men's. Recall that Butler postulated that the construction of masculinity requires that a man not only be attractive to women but also be attracted *to* them as well. As Wade (2017) explained, men's desire is central whilst women are positioned as objects to receive the desires of men, not as actors who experience their own desires beyond "wanting to be wanted" by men.[41] Shawn's and Sarah's experiences reveal that if a woman simply appears to be the type of woman that a man "should" be attracted to – traditionally gender conforming with Eurocentric features – then seemingly regardless of her sexual orientation (i.e. her desire) she is at risk of suffering from misdirected rebukes of colourism/sexual racism.

This early interpretation is supported by comments from River (35, US, Black/White, queer woman). Unlike Shawn and Sarah, River dresses in a more masculine manner. She also characterises her self-presentation as in line with punk rock and alternative styles. Unlike other interviewees, River was not bullied as an adolescent. She recalls:

> I never really felt like I experienced bullying. I mean, probably there was some rejection and probably people said mean stuff about me in high school but I just didn't really care ... if you're going to make fun of me for liking girls and wearing weird clothes, I don't care.

Unlike gender conforming women of various sexual orientations, River made no mention of "jealous" Black women harassing her for her appearance. Her experiences thus bolster the interpretation that straight Black women's rejection of colourism and sexual racism often gets misdirected towards those Black mixed-race women who are perceived, based on gender presentation and seemingly regardless of sexual orientation, to be attractive to straight (Black) men. Nevertheless, River identifies as mixed-race just like other Black mixed-race people in the sample. This suggests that whilst experiences within the heterosexual

---

[40]Candelario 2010.

[41]Wade 2017; In the aptly named chapter "Wanting to be wanted," Wade further explains that many heterosexual young women internalise their position as recipients of men's desire and come to view themselves through the male gaze. This self-objectification means that women "learn to focus on how they look [to men] instead of how they feel" (198), which can hinder their ability to experience physical pleasure during sexual encounters because they are so worried about how their body is being perceived by their partner.

matrix and Black community may differ by gender and sexual orientation, their influence, if any, on the racial identity of LGBTQIA mixed-race people is unclear.

Conclusion

Race, gender, sexuality, and other social systems operate synchronously, not independently. CMRS has examined these systems with respect to cisgender and heterosexual mixed-race people, and now scholars are beginning to do the same for mixed-race people who are LGBTQIA. Thus far, only one person in the UK has been interviewed for this study. Nevertheless, his account and the experiences of people like Michele Aboro, a mixed-race lesbian boxer from the UK,[42] indicates that there is fruitful ground for cross-cultural comparison. Further research could examine the similarities and differences between the US and UK mixed-race LGBTQIA populations as well as investigate how US/UK cultural exchange such as media, travel, studying abroad, etc., contribute to them. Such research would illuminate the role of context in how race, gender, and sexuality intersect to structure mixed-race people's experiences and contribute to their identity development.

Regarding Black mixed-race people in particular, the interviewees' accounts herein suggest that race, gender, and sexuality intersect in ways that both fit within as well as challenge heteronormative identity development theories. Previous theorisation about the role in racial identity development of acceptance or rejection from same gender Black peers appears to explain Black mixed-race gay men's experiences. Attention to queer women's experiences, on the other hand, presents a more nuanced view. In short, whilst it appears that extant theories are not completely inapplicable to the LGBTQIA population, there are unique aspects of mixedness that inattention to the full diversity of gender and sexual expression will continue to miss.

---

[42]Boerman and Reiziger 2004.

Chapter 8

Conclusion: Creating and Comparing a Mixed-Race Future

As we were finishing writing this book, the Duke and Duchess of Sussex welcomed a healthy baby boy, Archie Harrison Mountbatten-Windsor, into the Royal Family. As with their engagement, wedding, and pregnancy announcements, congratulations as well as reminders that mixed-race families and children will not cure institutionalised White supremacy immediately followed. For example, on the day that the Duke and Duchess had their first public posing with their newborn son, BBC DJ Danny Baker tweeted "Royal Baby leaves hospital," accompanied with a black-and-white photo of a well-dressed man and woman holding hands with a chimpanzee in a suit.[1] Despite Baker's claims of ignorance, there is a long history of racist tropes likening people with Black ancestry to primates. In addition, micro-aggressive commentary continues to frame the choices the Duke and Duchess make for their family as problematic or trouble-causing, including their refraining from giving their son the official Royal courtesy title of Earl of Dumbarton or Lord, and electing to keep their son's christening private.[2] In short, neither the Duchess nor Master Archie being mixed-race protects them from White supremacist discourse.

The Sussex family offers examples of many of the themes in this book. As discussed in Chapter 2, Archie is part of a growing population of mixed-race people in the US and UK. However, as noted in Chapter 3, despite recent changes to allow mixed-race identification, neither the US's "mark one or more" directive nor the UK's Mixed ethnicity category is a panacea. Because Meghan is of Black US American heritage, neither the UK's White and Black African nor the White and Black Caribbean categories accurately describe little Archie. He will thus, as Sims' UK interviewee Mary said of her heritage, likely have to mark "Any other Mixed background." In short, he, like many mixed-race people in the UK, continues to be othered within the new category.

---

[1]BBC News 2019; Greenfield and Badshah 2019.
[2]Gillett 2019; Greenspan 2019; Newsround 2019; Petter 2019.

Mixed-Race in the US and UK: Comparing the Past, Present, and Future, 103–108
Copyright © 2020 by Jennifer Patrice Sims and Chinelo L. Njaka
Published under exclusive licence
doi:10.1108/978-1-78769-553-520191009

Heeding Mahtani's warning that "a focus on individual's personal experience of race on a day-to-day level can actually work to obscure structural racism,"[3] in Chapters 4 through 7 we attempted to move beyond individual understandings and experiences of mixedness. Chapter 4 analysed the discourse of mixed-race civil society and reveals that, in the US, civil society organisations (CSOs) tend to rely on strict, biological understandings of mixed-race, whilst UK-based CSOs have begun to adopt more flexible and fluid constructions for their work. Mixed-Race people's common experience of being asked about their race and what those social experiences and the linguistic exchanges that characterise them reveals about status hierarchies, public space, the symbolic power of language, and community building were addressed in Chapter 5. How the Sussexes will teach Archie to navigate these mixed-race experiences will depend quite a lot on what he grows to look like. As discussed in Chapters 6 and 7, his racial identity will develop from a complex interplay of nature and nurture at the intersection of race, nationality, gender, physical appearance, sexuality, and more.

Comparing the Past, Present, and Future

Given the shared history, it might be expected that there would be parallels in the racial formation processes of the US and UK. Indeed, both countries made census enumeration changes that allowed for mixed-race categorisation during the same census cycle. This occurred within a simultaneous, relational shift to increased focus on mixed-race identity and experience in both nations, which thus fostered popular national discussions of mixed-race and provided the space for the development of mixed-race civil society. However, at the state, organisational, and individual levels, the similarities of mixed-race we found were largely superficial.

At the state level, both the US and the UK create and fix notions of race. An important place that this occurs is via the census, which does not merely describe demographic data, but produces discourses that function to construct specific racialisations of mixedness.[4]

Mixed-Race civil society, at the organisational level, tends to construct mixed-race as a fluid conception that can include elements of more than one racialised, ethnic, and/or national identity. "Mixed-Race" is not necessarily confined to the racialised categories prescribed by the census. Although most of the UK CSOs view mixed-race as a fluid concept, a minority focussed specifically on Black/White mixed-race. For these particular CSOs, they did not adopt a distinction between the "White and Black Caribbean" and the "White and Black African" racialised categories, as the UK Office for National Statistics (ONS) does. Rather, they were more rigid in their constructions of mixed-race, in that they conceptualised it based on the broad, racialised categories of "Black" and "White." The US Office of Management and Budget (OMB) categories were largely accepted by US mixed-race civil society as a basis

---

[3]Mahtani 2014: 245.
[4]Anderson 1991; Kertzer and Arel 2002; Nobles 2002.

for their conceptions of race. Most of the civil society organisation representatives interviewed offered that "race is a social construction," but despite this, many utilised biological paradigms of race to construct mixed-race and justify the need for their CSOs. Two organisations in particular expressed post-race desires to see an end to racialised categorisation eventually, and this position exposes the tension inherent in the use of racialised categories whilst wanting to be rid of them. Though UK mixed-race civil society at times cited US media as influential in their ideas of mixed-race, US mixed-race civil society was more insular and mentioned only US media and political influences in their work.

At the micro-level, mixed-race people in the US and the UK presently have similar day-to-day experiences. Filling out race details on forms is not a straightforward, tick-one-and-done as it is for so many others in the population; and mundane shopping trips can quickly become frustrating when strangers abruptly remind mixed-race people that their existence does not fit neatly into White western understandings of race. And yet, in both nations mixed-race people are not wholly circumscribed by these macro-level forces. Mixed-Race people creatively exercise agency and they often, like Du Bois, refuse to utter the expected words when implicitly asked what it feels like to be a problem.[5]

More interviewees in the US than UK reported being confrontational in these moments, which underscores that whilst mixed-race experiences may be similar due to transatlantic and indeed globalised conceptions of race, there are cultural specificities as well. The infamous one-drop rule continues to exert more influence over the self-identity of US Americans as well as mixed-race people of African descent in both nations, whereas challenges over origins, place, and belonging render the national identity of many in the UK precarious. How these identities are discussed, often in conversations abroad or by drawing explicit cross-national comparisons, is a reminder that international exchange, including exchange of ideas about (mixed-)race, is constantly occurring.

Looking towards the future, the US OMB and the UK ONS are both preparing for the next national census, scheduled for 2020 and 2021, respectively. The interstitial years between administering the census are not only for data analysis, but also for preparing for the next cycle. Part of the planning includes reviewing the specific questions to make sure they align with the topics on which the government wants to collect data. Additions, removals, and changes to questions are in response to the constantly shifting socio-political climate, with a stated aim to collect the most relevant information on each nation.

At the time of writing, the UK is still undergoing the consultation process for the 2021 census. Regarding the Ethnicity questions, an Arab category was introduced in 2011,[6] and the ONS received 55 requests from various stakeholder groups throughout the nation to add to or amend category options for the next census. The ONS has elected to pursue the requests relating to four groups:

---

[5]Du Bois 1903.
[6]Jivraj 2012; White 2012.

Roma, Somali, Sikh, and Jewish.[7] The format of the potential additions is being tested, with the possibility of Roma[8] and Jewish being added to either the White category or Other category, Somali being added to the Black category, and Sikh being added to either the Asian category or Other category. The result of these changes will impact the construction of Mixed or Multiple ethnicity, as the government will be officially acknowledging more ethnicity options from which respondents can choose.

Due to concerns about undercounting in previous cycles, the US Census Bureau has been considering changes to Census 2020. "Hispanic or Latino" may be changed from an ethnic category to a racial category. Another potential new racialised category to Census 2020 is the addition of a "Middle Eastern or North African" category.[9] In addition to these new racialised categories, the Census Bureau is also testing the provision of "origin" subcategories under each racialised category, as well as a place to write-in additional "details."[10] The new format will be similar to the structure of the previous Asian and Native Hawaiian or Other Pacific Islander options, though with the addition of clear race headings grouping the subcategories.

Census 2020 may also include a citizenship question, which has not been included on a US census since 1950. Although the census is conducted anonymously, the proposed addition is controversial, as it may negatively impact the response rates by US immigrants. Not only does underrepresentation lead to higher disproportionality of census differential undercounts, but it also hinders the ability of civil rights monitoring and funding for the most vulnerable groups. This may further affect the counts for the Two or More races population, especially considering the aforementioned proposed changes to the race and ethnicity questions. At the time of writing, the US Supreme Court has ruled against adding a question on citizenship in light of these concerns, however in response, the Trump administration is considering options either to bring the issue to court again with revised rationale or to use an executive order to mandate the question for Census 2020.[11]

The coming years will also see the next Critical Mixed Race Studies (CMRS) academic conference in 2021. The work on the social science side is heeding the call to move beyond simply "pointing out the socially constructed nature of race and the malleability of the racial experience for some (but of course not all) self-identified mixed-race people whose appearance is ambiguous."[12] Emerging research avenues are paying increased attention to the material consequences, for

---

[7]HM Government 2018.
[8]Testing has included a separate group for "Roma," as well as the extant "Gypsy or Irish Traveller" subgroup being renamed to "Romany Gypsy or Irish Traveller."
[9]Strmic-Pawl et al. 2018.
[10]Cohn 2017.
[11]Reuters 2019.
[12]Mahtani 2014: 244–245.

mixed-race populations and others, of changing constructions of race, and are investigating the implications of some mixed-race people's racial fluidity. In political science, researchers are analysing the identities of mixed-race people as they relate to political attitudes, and by logical extension, political behaviours such as voting as well.[13] Other political scientists are focussing on mixed-race people running for political office by using experiments to test voters' responses to mixed-race political candidates.[14] Legal scholars are also turning attention to the implications of how others view mixed-race people, explicating, for instance, how mixed-race people in the US are discriminated against in employment, education, housing, and the criminal justice system. In sum, as Hernández (2018) reminds us, the way forward towards racial justice "can only be done by shifting away from a focus on individual identity recognition to a focus on group-based racial realities."[15]

The spectre of racial discrimination and other unpleasant aspects of mixedness have been deemphasised as researchers have moved beyond the nineteenth and early twentieth centuries writings that pathologised mixed-race people. Nevertheless, as Black feminist scholars remind us, "in our quest to set the record straight," we must not "only focus on the strengths, accomplishments, and victories [for this] does not give sufficient attention to the system of domination."[16] In this book, we have shown that mixed-race people continue to suffer almost daily micro-aggressions and are at risk of racist violence at the hands of the state for one or more of their social identities. From White mixed-race children having lower rates of poverty than single- and double-minority race children in the US[17] to the fact that mixed-race children are disproportionately in foster care in the UK,[18] more research is needed from sociologists in both nations on how mixed-race people, despite the post-racial rhetoric, still suffer under White supremacist oppression.

On the flip side, both researchers and the public must take care to avoid the trap of overlooking when mixedness may be perpetuating harm. For one, scholars must not uncritically assume that changing racial boundaries creating a space for mixed-race automatically implies a change towards racial justice.[19] Additionally, scholars should be critical of the practical invisibly of mixed-race people who engage in nefarious activities. The high profile case of convicted rapist Daniel Holtzclaw, for instance, mostly ignored that he is mixed-race, despite racial identity overly dominating stories about mixed-race people when they have great successes. This discrepancy in visibility should make scholars and the public alike question whose purposes are being served when mixed-race identity is disproportionately afforded to the extraordinarily talented and positively accomplished.[20]

---

[13]Davenport 2018; Masuoka 2017.
[14]Lemi 2018.
[15]Hernández 2018: 126.
[16]Evens-Winters 2019; Mullings 1997.
[17]Bratter et al. 2013.
[18]Gov.uk 2019.
[19]Mahtani 2014; Masuoka 2017.
[20]Storti 2017.

Conclusion

Joining a nascent literature focussing on the US and UK, *Mixed-Race in the US and UK* combined macro- and micro-level analysis of the experiences of both political change-makers and the people on the ground who accept and challenge society's racialised boundaries. Employing both a comparativist and relational approach, we demonstrated how the census, racial identity, civil society, and everyday experiences at the intersection of race, gender, class, and sexuality are similar and different in the two nations and how shared historical events as well as contemporary connections influenced and continue to influence the observed patterns.

Methodologically, our research findings support arguments made by Stephen Small that systematic cross-national comparison is an important approach in the examination of racialisation processes.[21] Although superficially, "mixed-race" is understood approximately in the same ways in both nations, we found significant differences in the ways that it is officially constructed and experienced in the US and the UK. Examining the social processes at both the micro- and macro-levels of societies as well as examining how societies compare to and influence each other reveals nuances in the ways that race is conceived and operationalised. It also reveals that despite the contextually specific nuance of mixed-race, its ability to both challenge and exist within traditional White supremacist notions of race is transatlantic.

With regard to theory, as has been argued elsewhere,[22] whether considering governments' construction of official categories or the responses of frustrated individuals who have been asked "what are you"/ "where are you from" one too many times, mixed-race is an important location for the examination of race theorisation more broadly. There has been an increasing body of work within CMRS over the last two decades, however, within more general race theorisation, racialisation of mixed-race remains understudied as a particular focus. Subsequently, this remaining disconnect lessens the potential for generalised race theorisation to be informed and challenged by mixed-race studies.

We agree that it is necessary to be critical when considering "race" – carefully questioning assumptive labels and meanings. It not only reflects the social, historical, and political influences of society; it also reflects the power influences at work in society. These influences include the construction and categorisation of people groups, the rights that they are afforded, social opportunities and attainment, and discrimination. "Doing race" works in conjunction with structural-level influences, as we demonstrated by focussing on how mixed-race people who are perceived as ambiguous exercise power to shape race at the micro-level by asserting identity, responding to questions, and interacting with family and peers. As more research continues to use a race-critical lens, scholars will not only help to identify the ways in which race functions at different levels of society, but will continue to help promote social change and social justice.

---

[21]Bhattacharyya et al. 2002; Small 1994a, 2009; Small and King-O'Riain 2014.
[22]See, for example, Ali 2003; Garner 2010; Ifekwunigwe 2004; Parker and Song 2001.

Methodological Appendix

Conducting Qualitative Research on Both Sides of the Atlantic

Hi, I'm Chinelo –
I was not expecting you to sound like that! Where's your accent from? Canada?
Close, it's from the US.
What? I was expecting a Nigerian accent! So, you went there before coming here [to the UK], I see.
No, I was born there.
Right, your parents immigrated there before you were born.
My dad did. My mom is from the US.
She's White?
Well – she doesn't consider herself White, no. She identifies as Black.
Ah, you're [US] American! Cool. So, when are you going back?

The above dialogue (and many versions of it!) are common for the second author, whereby the salience of racialisation and nationality often intersect in her everyday experience whilst living in the UK. This conversation occurred at the beginning of one of her interviews with a representative from a UK mixed-race civil society organisation (CSO). Her accent betraying her, the first order of business became pinning down the unasked question of identity and assuaging the increasing confusion as the dialogue progressed. It was laden with incorrect assumptions until satisfaction was finally reached, only then to switch focus to immigration status – yet another salient issue in the UK context, especially when anti-immigration sentiments were rising in political discourse in the years leading up to the UK referendum to leave the European Union. The account shows brilliantly how mixed-race is conceptualised in the UK in contrast to the US for, as discussed in earlier chapters, it exemplifies how race, nationality, ethnicity, and culture are more often part of discussions – and qualitative research – on mixed-race in the UK than in the US.

This Methodological Appendix begins with an in-depth accounting of each author's research methods. Following that it offers a discussion of the processes, challenges, and benefits of conducting qualitative research in two countries drawing on both research literatures as well as the authors' own assessment from first-hand research experiences. It concludes by looking beyond the US and UK specifically to provide insights into conducting multinational qualitative research in general.

Researching Mixed-Race at the Macro and Organisational Levels: Dr Njaka's Research

Chapters 2 and 4 are based on Dr Njaka's qualitative research. The study used a combination of critical discourse analysis (CDA) and interview data in order to examine mixed-race constructions by states and mixed-race civil society in the US and the UK. Facet methodology allowed for the strategic use of multiple approaches to illuminate different aspects – or facets – of different but related lines of inquiry. This methodology assumes that the social world is multidimensional, yet entwined. As such, multiple methods used together provide a fuller data set with which to reveal and analyse racialised construction processes within my research sites.[1]

Research Sites

My research centred on the addition of mixed-race as a racialised option on the US and UK censuses; therefore, I used 2000 and 2010 census data from the US Census Bureau and Office of Management and Budget (OMB), and 2001 and 2011 census data from the UK's Office for National Statistics (ONS).[2] I used mixed-race CSOs as organisational-level research sites. The organisation profiles, including overviews of what each does and the specific people with which each work, can be found below. The particularities of the various bodies are wide ranging, but the similarity among the groups that I queried is that they organise themselves based on the commonality of a constructed notion of "mixed-race."

Mixed-Race Discourses

For both types of mixed-race racial formation projects, I examined the discourses about mixed-race that were generated in both settings and used to describe and construct mixed-race. Following Suki Ali, I use the Foucauldian concept of discourse that explains it as text "that create[s] and construct[s] the fields and institutions they seek to explicate and serve."[3] This definition acknowledges the conveying of information (knowledge), and that the sources for this type of discourse must have some ability (power) to do so.

I focussed on two types of racial projects, with the assumption that they would produce differing discourses on mixed-race. I also assumed that there were likely some overlap and linkages between the two types of sources, in which I was also interested. Discourses are localised texts, in that they are specific to particular times, spaces, and social contexts; and furthermore, communicate

---

[1]Mason 2011.
[2]The UK census data was limited to England and Wales. Chapter 2 gives further details.
[3]Ali 2003: 30; Foucault 1978.

Table A1.   Profiles of Mixed-Race CSOs.

US-Based Representative(s)	CSO Overview
Holly	Three interrelated organisations based in a major city. The first provides training for the parents (particularly White parents) in transracial adoptive families. The second is a local affiliate of a national group that has been prominent in the national campaign to allow for mixed-race categorisation on the US census. The third is a social group for mixed-race people. Each group is led by a small team of people and reaches participants in the hundreds. The second and third groups target Black/White mixed-race individuals and families, however they are not exclusive to that demographic.
Graeme	Organisation provides training, publications, and educational resources; predominantly targeted towards professionals in primary, secondary, and tertiary education. Led by Graeme, his reach is in the hundreds for the trainings and estimated thousands for his numerous publications. The focus of the group is open to any mixed-race demographic, however the usual focus is on Black/White mixed-race.
Denise	One of the national groups that campaigned for mixed-race representation on the US census, specifically through the addition of a single mixed-race category. Additionally, they campaign for a mixed-race category on all government, educational, and other monitory forms in the US. The organisation is led by a small team and have a national reach of parents and families estimated to be in the tens of thousands. Sister organisation to the one run by Courtney.
Courtney	One of the national groups that campaigned for mixed-race representation on the US census, specifically through the addition of a single mixed-race category. Focussing specifically on outreach with mixed-race teenagers and young adults, the small leadership team mobilises campaigns for representation on official monitoring forms and mixed-race registration for bone marrow donation. Sister organisation to the one run by Denise.
Trevor	National (with limited international reach) organisation that promotes "multicultural" community from all backgrounds and racialised designations. The small team supports the planning of local events in multiple locations throughout the US to celebrate and commemorate the national legalisation of interracial marriage. Thousands of individuals and families are estimated to participate throughout the year.

Table A1. (*Continued*)

US-Based Representative(s)	CSO Overview
Qianru	A small team produces an approximately quarterly national magazine focussing on Asian and Mixed Asian (domestic and abroad) issues and commentary. They have a modest subscriber base (less than 1,000), but the reach is estimated to be above that when including their supporting web and social media presence.

UK-Based Representative(s)	CSO Overview
Xavier	Founder Xavier develops educational materials, trainings, and community fora for teenaged mixed-race students with Black and White parentage. He also mentors teenagers to further develop and faciliatate trainings for their peers. The programmes run nation-wide, though largely concentrated in northern England. Several hundred students have been involved in the school trainings and around 50 students have participated in mentorship programmes.
Linda	Internet-based community and support forum specifically for Black/White mixed-race teenagers and adults. Though there is community participation and posting, content (news, opinion, and reports) is primarily curated by Linda. Users are from around the UK and abroad, and the website averages around 10,000 hits per month.
Neela	A small, local community social and support group set up in southwestern England in partnership with local government. They meet regularly to talk about and explore their experiences of mixedness, particularly in their undiverse area. Any self-identified mixed-race individuals or interracial families are welcome to attend. About 10–15 families are involved regularly, with approximately 40 adults and children in attendance at each meeting.
Jemima	A local organisation, run by a small team, that provides care for young children (up to five-years-old) in a multicultural borough in London. In addition to providing care for children, the organisation provides support and training for parents, including immigration, job-seeking, and liasing with local services as relevant. Approximately 100 children participate in the programme.

Table A1.   (*Continued*)

UK-Based Representative(s)	CSO Overview
Valaria Stephen	A local, small team-run organisation located within a multicultural borough in London. The organisation provides care for young children under the age of five, and provides limited support for their parents. The organisation has under 100 children in participation.
Femilola	A mental health services organisation located in a multicultural borough in London. Led by a small team, the organisation does outreach and provides mental health trainings, workshops, support, and monitoring for Black and Minority Ethnic adults, aged 18–65; many of whom identify as mixed-race. Additionally, they provide diversity/cultural training to voluntary and statutory organisations. On average, 25–50 adults attend the outreaches, and they have a caseload of around 50 adults.
Dienke	An organisation based in southeastern England that faciliates training and support for transracial adoptive parents, including those adopting mixed-race children. A small team provides and facilitates support though training, family therapies, community with other adoptive families and liases with external local services as needed. The organisation manages a caseload of 20–30 families at a given time, and have served hundreds throughout its operation.

that particularity to express and understand human experiences in that locality.[4] Thus, discursive texts are versatile sources for analysing the language, culture, social institutions; and the assumptions and environments from which they come. Discourses cover a variety of areas of life and therefore are not confined to a specific type of text.[5] For this reason, I selected census report and policy documents and interview texts as primary data sources. Particularly for the interview texts, I wanted to make sure to use forms of data that are interpersonal in nature. As Donald Polkinghorne posits, "[s]tories express a kind of knowledge that uniquely describes human experience[,] and actions and happenings contribute positively and negatively to attaining goals and fulfilling

[4]Ali 2003; Tyson 1999; Whisnant 2009.
[5]Foucault 1972; Whisnant 2009.

purposes."[6] The unique knowledge that is contained and conveyed in narrative forms of dialogue is worth analysing to explore the inner-workings of institutions and organisations.

In the interview process, the articulated knowledge is both narrative and paradigmatic in nature.[7] Therefore, this type of generated discourse was useful alongside the other sources for examining descriptions and conceptions of mixed-race more deeply, through the process of interaction. There are undoubtedly other forms of texts that I could have selected to analyse these discourses, but my chosen data sources are satisfactory in that their intended audience are those outside of the organisations.

With "discourse" comes implied "power" and "knowledge," as mentioned above. Foucault[8] argues that discourse is not necessarily linear or uniform, but rather varying elements work with (or against) each other in the struggle for power and knowledge. In examining different types of discourses from differing sites across two nations, I used the various texts as means to examine the different types of knowledge and power that is generated, accepted, and contested. I was interested in the similarities between and among the macro-level and organisational-level bodies and their national contexts. I was also interested in the differences, inconsistencies, and contestations across the specific elements of discourse. I aimed to understand in more sophisticated detail the nuances in the constructions of mixed-race across these sites, which became apparent through the use of discursive texts from differing sites.

Census Data Collection and Analysis

My research used a novel qualitative approach to analyse national census outputs. Quantitative approaches are nearly the exclusive approach for census organisations to assess mixed-race categorisation in both countries.[9] That being said, there are a few examples of qualitative analyses used to research census outcomes and implications.[10] My qualitative research aimed to contribute to the existing body of quantitative census data and associated research on race and racialisation. Instead of duplicating methodology to analyse census responses, I positioned my research in an alternative direction and "analysed the analyses."

---

[6]Polkinghorne 1995: 9.

[7]Polkinghorne 1995.

[8]Foucault 1978: 100 states that "Indeed, it is in discourse that power and knowledge are joined together. And for this very reason, we must conceive discourse as a series of discontinuous segments whose tactical function is neither uniform nor stable. To be more precise, we must not imagine a world of discourse divided between accepted discourse and excluded discourse, or between the dominant discourse and the dominated one; but as a multiplicity of discursive elements that can come into play in various strategies."

[9]Denscombe 2007.

[10]Ballard 1996; Hainer 1987.

I aimed to examine the ways in which mixed-race is conceptualised and constructed by two nation states by both looking at the reporting of census results by census bodies and at the conclusions they draw about mixed-race in the process.

I analysed official reports published by the OMB (on behalf of the US Census Bureau) and the ONS for the descriptions, conceptions, and constructions of mixed-race populations. The research focussed on the 2000 and 2010 US censuses and the UK 2001 and 2011 censuses of England and Wales. Beginning the research with these analyses also helped to provide an overview and context for the following analyses of mixed-race CSOs detailed in the following section.

I collected the publications made available from the US Census Bureau and ONS websites that discussed census findings relating broadly to "cultural demographics" (e.g. race, ethnicity and religion), as well as "socioeconomic demographics" (e.g. education and employment data). I conducted a CDA starting from the main publications overviewing race and ethnicity and mixed-race populations. CDA is a particular analytical approach that examines the relationship between authority and the use of language.[11] The primary purpose of these census publications is to provide public users (e.g. researchers, community organisations, students, and individuals) a way to learn more about the justification for the national census, the information that is collected, the process by which it is collected, a summary and interpretation of the information, and the uses of this information in the governance of each country.[12]

I also had the opportunity to interview employees of the census organisations. The communications included telephone and electronic message queries to both the US Census Bureau and ONS customer services departments. In both cases, these customer services departments are especially set up to assist members of the public to access information on the censuses and obtain publications and other data products. Through the advice of customer services representatives, as well as personal contacts at the University of Manchester, I was able to access employees working for the ONS on the 2011 census consultation. I attended a consultation meeting at the ONS where primarily academic users of census data were providing feedback on the proposed ethnicity questions for the 2011 census. Following the meeting, I was able to communicate further with two workers: informally with one and a semi-structured interview with the other. Through these various interactions, I was able to ask specific questions that I had about the census process in the UK. I was also able to obtain information about the official ethnic categories used on the 2001 census and the coding practices used in processing and analysing the census responses. Finally, I was also able to seek clarification and additional information about areas of ambiguity I found in the census discourse.

---

[11]Fairclough 2010; Keller 2013; van Dijk 1993, 2001.
[12]Grieco and Cassidy 2001; Jones and Bullock 2012; ONS 2012a; Rendall 2005.

Mixed-Race Civil Society Data Collection and Analysis

I continued a qualitative approach for the examination of mixed-race civil society in the US and UK. I used the accounts of representatives, in their CSO work and personal anecdotes, to examine the ways that they and their organisations conceptualise notions of and construct mixed-race. I began researching mixed-race civil society using current literature around the topic, personal communications and the internet. From the literature and a personal communication, I knew that there have been estimates of current and active mixed-race CSOs numbered in the 70s in the US in the latter half of the 2000s decade.[13] I could not find any literature giving estimates in the UK. I assumed that the number would be significantly smaller due to a smaller national population size and the differing histories around advocacy. I sought a range of organisations in order to capture a scope of community, support, advocacy and policy goals of the various organisations in both nations. For my purposes, the organisations I sought were confined to those that work primarily with mixed-race individuals and interethnic/interracial families, and initially did not include organisations with a primary focus of transracial adoption. This was because I wanted to confine my focus to organisational descriptions and conceptions of individuals constructed as "mixed-race." Whilst transracial adoption does work with individuals categorised as such, in most cases, this is only a part of the wider demographic accessing transracial adoption agencies. These agencies typically have a general focus on families where the children are of differing racialised classifications to their adoptive parent(s), rather than specifically reflecting racialised mixedness. However, when transracial adoption was included in the focusses along with mixed-race individuals and/or interracial families, the organisation was included for further analyses.

I conducted an in-depth content analysis of printed and electronic media (e.g. organisation websites, newsletters, policy briefs, etc.) for approximately 15–20 organisations for each country, in order to gain a preliminary understanding of the varying types of organisations, as well as to begin to uncover the recurrent discourse of mixed-race organisations to the public. The texts from these printed media were analysed thematically by coding relevant keywords and themes, and finding relationships among them.

Following the content analysis, I approached around 13–15 of the mixed-race CSOs for each country for further research. I decided on potential CSOs by considering their specific focus(ses), the information available, the frequency of key themes addressed in a document analysis, and accessibility. My aim was to have every theme represented in the organisations I approached, but this was not always possible. For example, I identified Hapa groups in the US, however I did not identify any Hapa groups based in the UK. Additionally, through this method, organisations that operated in relative isolation or without internet-based promotional tools were more likely to be missed in the content analysis than organisations with a stronger online presence. A further factor that was outside of my control was the availability of CSO representatives. Through a

---

[13]DaCosta 2007; Hochschild 2007; Williams 2005, 2006.

combination of representativeness and availability, this yielded seven organisations based in the UK and six organisations based in the US that agreed to participate in semi-structured interviews.

Following requests for permission to participate, I conducted semi-structured interviews either in person or by telephone with at least one individual in a position of leadership within each organisation between 2008 and 2011. The interview schedule began with asking questions about the CSO and its scope, then moved to how the organisation defined "mixed-race," how the organisation fit into wider mixed-race civil society, and how the CSO used census categories and/or data in its work. Each of the US interviews were with only one person. For the UK organisations, there were two instances where there was more than one interviewee: one interview was with two representatives and another was mainly with one, though five other colleagues were in the office during the interview and offered insight off and on as CSO representatives. Two of the six interviews were in person for the US organisations, and five of the seven were in person for the UK organisations. I decided to focus on participants in leadership positions because of the nature of my inquiry; a person or persons in leadership would be comfortable and familiar with speaking from that position of leadership about the organisation and the participants. I found this approach to be the most appropriate because leadership is part of power/knowledge and discourse, and it is from this positioning that I am examining in my research. This generally did not create any problems except for those of availability and accessibility. On occasion, it was difficult to coordinate interviews due to the organisations not having the capacity to do so, or the necessary individuals telling me that they were "too busy" to speak with me (assumed to be a polite way to express disinterest). Another factor that I believe influenced a small number of potential organisations was a suspicion of the interview process itself – my being unknown to them or being sceptical of academic researchers due to previous experiences. I gathered this from some "shutdown" I received when I mentioned my interview requests, as well as an "anti-academy" suspicion articulated to me by some of the respondents. Others asked questions of me at the beginning of the interview to learn more about me and my "research motives." Only when they were satisfied with my answers and comfortable opening up to me were we able to shift to my interview questions.

Some of the interviewees requested anonymity. In order to safeguard against identification (in particular, by omission), I elected to anonymise all interview participants by assigning pseudonyms and withholding the specific names and locations of the CSOs.

The interview schedule was informed by the aforementioned content analyses of printed resources and the census analyses. I conducted the interviews with the aim of collecting data specifically about the ways each mixed-race CSO describe and conceptualise – and therefore construct – mixedness and "mixed-race people," the overall goals and missions of the organisation and the specific work they do to address any areas of social inequality and disadvantage referred to in their discourses, and on how the census and the state influence or otherwise affect the work of their organisations.

I used framework analysis[14] to analyse the transcribed interview data through a race-critical lens.[15] The transcribed interviews were indexed and synthesised thematically, using themes both from the previous analysis on mixed-race CSOs and those that emerged from the interviews themselves. As the interview schedule was somewhat thematic in terms of the order questions were asked, some of the thematic categories were also initially developed by using the interview schedule as a guide for thematic generation. The thematic indices and syntheses were then used to identify key themes in each transcript, as well as identify links between the themes among the organisations within and across national contexts. From the thematic analysis, I developed representational generalised findings from the gathered interview data in order to understand how mixed-race organisations understand and communicate "mixed-race," and how they support "mixed-race" individuals and families within each national context.[16]

Researching Mixed-Race at the Micro-Level: Dr Sims' In-Depth Interview Studies

The data and analysis in Chapters 3, 5, 6, and 7 are based on Dr Sims' in-depth interview studies. The first study was conducted from 2011 to 2014. It examined the impact of looking "racially ambiguous" on mixed-race individuals' daily experiences (e.g. dealing with questions such as "what are you?" or "where are you from?") and racial identity development.[17] In response to the heteronormativity of this first study, a second project focussing exclusively on Lesbian, Gay, Bisexual, Transgender, Queer, Intersex, and Asexual (LGBTQIA) mixed-race people was begun in 2018.

Due to absence of population "membership" lists from which to sample randomly, targeted recruitment online and offline is a normative sampling method in Critical Mixed Race Studies. Online recruitment for participation in offline data collection is a recent technique.[18] This method of recruitment has a number of advantages, however, most importantly it allows the researcher to locate members of the targeted population who have had the specific experience or who possess the specific characteristics of theoretical interest.

For my first study, I utilised the internet to recruit mixed-race adults from mixed-race organisations' websites and from social network sites. In 2011, I advertised for participants through the UK organisation People In Harmony, on the British web-community Intermix, and in a Facebook group called "Mixed-Race UK." Recruitment of US participants began in 2012 by posting or emailing research advertisements via the following local affiliates of the Association of Multi-Ethnic Americans: IPride, The Biracial Family Network, and Multiracial Americans of Southern California. In all cases, the

---

[14]Ritchie and Lewis 2003.
[15]Essed and Goldberg 2002.
[16]Denscombe 2007; Richie and Lewis 2003.
[17]See Sims 2016 and Sims and Joseph-Salisbury 2019.
[18]Hirsch et al. 2014.

advertisement included asking if the reader is often asked "what race are you" or "where are you from" in order to ensure a theoretical sample of not just mixed-race participants but mixed-race participants who are perceived by others to be phenotypically racially ambiguous. My second study on LGBTQIA mixed-race people began in 2018 and is recruiting participants almost exclusively via social media (mainly Twitter). Due to retweets and word of mouth, prospective participants email to express interest in participating in the study. Whilst a limitation of internet-based recruitment is that it is biased in favour of internet users, it is nonetheless especially useful for cross-national research because it holds recruitment constant across cases by sampling among the same sub-population of mixed-race people (online community members) in both nations.

Despite the development of internet recruiting, snowball sampling (i.e. direct solicitation of people who are members of the research population with the request that they refer other population members as potential participants as well) from offline personal and professional contacts remains a widely used recruitment method for research with mixed-race populations. Whilst in London in 2011, I asked friends, colleagues, and new acquaintances if they knew a mixed-race person who might be willing to sit for an interview. Additionally, having learned from early interviewees (e.g. Dave) that light skinned people of colour in the UK are more likely to be mixed-race than light skinned people of colour in the US, I also recruited participants by asking light skinned people of colour I met (e.g. Dean and Emma) if they happened to be mixed-race. All were, and two-thirds agreed to an interview. Many US research participants were located via snowball sampling, too. I asked colleagues, family, and friends if they knew any mixed-race people who would be willing to participate and then called, texted, emailed, or Facebook messaged those who were interested. All but one person agreed to be interviewed.

Data Collection

Interview guides were the data collection tool for these studies. For the first study, the guide began by establishing racial background, racial identity, and early racial socialisation, before asking about experiences with questions such as "where are you from" or "what are you" due to having an ambiguous physical appearance. The third set of questions pertained to the practice and effects of bodywork such as hair styling, tanning, piercings, and tattooing that may alter or influence perceived racialised appearance. The LGBTQIA study interview guide included questions on these topics as well as additional questions on sexual and gender identity and socialisation, bullying, friendships, and relationships. Both interview guides ended with questions about the future and requests for additional demographic information (e.g. age and socioeconomic status), and the LGBTQIA study asked a final question about best practices for protecting LGBTQIA youth who want to participate in social science research. Finally, the guides close by offering interviewees an opportunity to ask questions about me or the research.

Using the interview guides, data were collected via semi-structured in-depth interviews with 30 mainly heterosexual mixed-race adults (first study) and, as of this writing, 16 LGBTQIA older adolescents and adults (second study). Interviews ranged from 30 minutes to an hour and a half and were conducted by me in the location of the participant's choice or via telephone or internet (e.g. Skype). The most popular physical locations in both nations included but were not limited to: cafes, coffee shops, bars, and restaurants.[19] For both studies, I offered to buy interviewees a drink or meal when meeting in food service venues. In addition, due to having university research funds by the time of the second study, all LGBTQIA study participants were also offered 10 US dollars for their time.

Samples

In the first study, of the 30 interviewees, 12 were in the UK and 18 were in the US. Eleven were men and 19 were women, all cisgender. The racial composition of the sample is: 18 Black/White interviewees, six Asian/White interviewees, two Asian/Black interviewees, one Black/Latino interviewee, one Native American/White interviewee, and two multiracial interviewees. Two respondents, one man and one woman, identified as bisexual; all other interviewees (28) identified as heterosexual. The age range spans from 19 to 49. Half of the UK sample described their family of origin as middle class and half described it as working class or between working class and middle class. In the US, the majority of the interviewees (10 of 18) described their families as middle class. Six said their families were "poor" or "lower middle" class; and two said their families were "upper middle" class.

Of the first 16 interviewees for my LGBTQIA study, 14 were in the US (though one was a Canadian currently visiting in the US), one was in the UK, and one was in South Africa. Eight are women (seven cis, one trans), seven are men (all cis), and one is non-binary. The racial composition of these first interviewees is: six Black/White, five Asian/White, three Mexican/White, and two multiracial. Spanning ages 15–50 (with a median and mode in the late 20s), the majority (nine) identified as gay or lesbian. Regarding the socioeconomic status of their family of original, two interviewees said they were "poor;" nine said they were "lower income," "lower middle," or "working class;" and five said they were "middle" or "upper middle" class.

---

[19]Interestingly, though the locations were similar in the two nations the process of selecting them differed. In UK, interviewees often gave me an exact address for our meeting whereas in the US interviewees wanted me to tell them where to show up. Whether this represents differential interview norms in each nation or differential assumptions about how well I knew their cities, it underlies the fact that conducting qualitative research in two contexts necessitates being adaptive as protocol patterns may need to shift or, as in this case, reverse completely.

Table A2.   Dr Sims' Study 1 Sample Characteristics.

		Sample Characteristics			
Name	**Nation**	**Gender**	**Age**	**Racial Backround**	**Racial Identity**
Dave	UK	Male	30	Black/White	Black or Mixed
Mary	UK	Female	41	Asian/White	Mixed
George	UK	Male	41	Asian/Black	Black
Sara	UK	Female	38	Black/White	Mixed
Dean	UK	Male	27	Black/White	Black
Smith	UK	Male	25	Asian/White	Mixed
Sophie	UK	Female	22	Black/White	Mixed
Emma	UK	Female	22	Asian/White	Mixed ("White Asian")
Vincent	UK	Male	36	Black/White	Black or Mixed
Lisa	UK	Female	40	Black/White	Mixed
Fleur	UK	Female	34	Black/White	Mixed
Claire	UK	Female	40	Asian/White	Mixed
Larell	US	Male	22	Black/White	Black
Carmen	US	Female	31	Asian/Black/Latino/White	Black
Sally	US	Female	19	Asian/White	Filipino
Sydney	US	Female	39	Black/White	Mixed ("Multiracial")
Joy	US	Female	27	Black/White	Black
Annette	US	Female	31	Black/White	Mixed
Heather	US	Female	25	Asian/Black	Mixed ("Chamaican") or Black
Judy	US	Female	30	Black/White	Black
Bo	US	Male	36	Black/White	Black
Suzie	US	Female	33	Black/White	Black
Aaliyah	US	Female	25	Black/White	Mixed ("Biracial")
Frost	US	Male	28	Black/Latino	Black
Tia	US	Female	37	Native American/Black/White	Black or Mixed
Chris	US	Male	30	Black/White	Black

Table A2.   (*Continued*)

Sample Characteristics					
Name	**Nation**	**Gender**	**Age**	**Racial Backround**	**Racial Identity**
Jennifer	US	Female	34	Black/White	Mixed or Other
Mark	US	Male	49	Native American/ White	Mixed
Anna	US	Female	24	Asian/White	Person of Colour/ Non-White
John	US	Male	25	Black/White	Black

Data Analysis

Digital audio recordings were taken during all interviews, and they were tran-scribed verbatim by me (nine) and a professional transcriptionist (37). Data were analysed both inductively and deductively in the qualitative data analysis soft-ware program NVivo. Analysis began by creating a node (i.e. code) for each of the main questions that were asked during data collection, and I used them to code interviewees' answers to each main question. I next examined the data pertain-ing to each node in turn to define what was happening and what it meant to the interviewees.[20] Concepts and processes were noted by creating sub-nodes under each main node. Sub-nodes were generated inductively until they accounted for all variation in the data. After thematically grouping the sub-nodes, I looked for similarities and differences across sub-groups of interviewees by characteristics such as race, gender, and nationality. I calculated simple descriptive statistics of emergent themes, such as tallying the per cent of interviewees with various char-acteristics who manifested particular sub-nodes.

In addition to this inductive analysis, because categories like race, class, and gender are "ongoing interactional accomplishments," I also deductively analysed the data for manifestations of "doing difference."[21] During the deductive analysis, I coded the data for interactions including but not limited to what constitutes a "successful" or "unsuccessful" accomplishment of race and in what context and with what consequences does one "do" race in a certain manner.

Though in previous publications[22] I labelled my inductive process as grounded theory analysis[23] and considered it separate from my deductive analysis process, Deterding and Waters (2018) description of "flexible coding" is a more accurate description of my analysis processes as a unified whole. From their review of cur-rent conventions in qualitative sociology, their own work on numerous qualitative

---

[20]Charmaz 2006.
[21]West and Fenstermaker 1995.
[22]Sims 2016, 2018; Sims and Joseph-Salisbury 2019.
[23]Charmaz 2006; Glaser and Strauss 1967.

projects, and their "informal discussions with contemporary researchers using large-scale interview data," they conclude that few contemporary qualitative sociologists actually implement the processes of grounded theory data collection and analysis as laid out by Glaser and Strauss (1967).[24] The availability of qualitative data analysis software as well as "practical demands of modern academic life" such as Institutional Review Board and grant applications which require literature reviews and research questions/hypothesis, "all run contrary to" pure grounded theory.[25] The modified "flexible coding" that I and many qualitative sociologists are in fact actually doing consists of conducting semi-structured interviews with samples of $N > 30$ that are analysed via "some combination of induction and literature- or theory-based coding" in order to relate independent and dependant variables to one another.[26]

With regard to themes by nation, racial group, gender, etc., I took both a comparative and a relational approach. On the comparative side, I tallied within themes to discover if interviewees of a particular identity (e.g. mixed-race heritages, gender, nationality, class, etc.) discussed them more or less frequently than others. As discussed in Chapter 3, for instance, understanding one's racial identities in tandem with national identities was a theme that was more prevalent in UK than US interviewees' accounts. As revealed in Chapter 7, by contrast, the same types of experiences with peers were equally prevalent in the data of women of different sexual orientations.

Taking a relational approach involved attempting to make sense of the observed differences and similarities by situating them in historic context and contemporary interrelation. The fact that Black mixed-race people in both nations were more constrained in their identity options than non-Black mixed-race people is a vestige of both nations' history with the enslavement and rigid classification of Africans in the early modern period. A relational approach also means paying attention to the results of the simple fact that people move and talk to other people in other places. As revealed by Sara's conversation with a woman whilst on holiday in Turkey (Chapter 5), when mixed-race people move they "carry their ways of seeing race with them ... discover new ways of seeing themselves and others ... [and] encourage others to expand their understandings."[27] Conversations and confrontations with others are thus moments where different racial understandings are coming into contact with and learning from one another.

Conducting Qualitative Research on Both Sides of the Atlantic: Processes, Challenges, and Benefits

When conducting qualitative research in multiple contexts, one will not have a consistent position vis-à-vis all interviewees. In our interviews with both US- and

---

[24]Deterding and Waters 2018: 5.
[25]Deterding and Waters 2018: 5.
[26]Deterding and Waters 2018: 13.
[27]Mills 2017: 246.

UK-based interviewees, for instance, perceptions[28] of our nationality and race, as well as our status as academics, marked us as outsiders to some and insiders to others. This positionality influenced the research process from the recruitment stage onward. Having differing, sometimes opposite, types of processes at play during research is a challenge for obtaining comparable quality data in both contexts. Nevertheless, being aware, reflexive, and adaptive can allow a researcher to capitalise on the benefits of inconsistent positionality and can help avoid the drawbacks.

"We're in England": Processes, Challenges, and Benefits of Outsider Status

Regarding nationality, the perception of the researcher as an outsider can influence recruitment to the study. Early on Dr Njaka noticed differences in accessibility when speaking with civil service employees working with census data in the US and UK in that she experienced more reluctance and suspicion from the UK-based interviewees than the interviewees based in the US. In attempting to speak to three civil service employees in the UK, only two responded to her initial enquiries. One organisation that was e-mailed for an interview replied that they "did not have the resources to help at this time." As the request was simply to speak to a representative about their organisation, this can be seen as a polite expression of disinterest.

Both of the UK census organisation representatives that agreed to interviews were tentative and somewhat reticent in their telephone communications. One employee did not remember Dr Njaka from their previous meeting and seemed suspicious of the research questions and her interest in the census process. A second employee, who she had met on two different prior occasions, remembered Dr Njaka when they spoke on the telephone and yet still seemed nervous, which was different from his demeanour during their previous encounters. This nervousness persisted at the beginning of interviews, manifesting as interviewees being cautious with their responses.

Whereas when US-based organisations presented some difficulty during the recruitment stage of the process it typically stemmed from their weariness at being inundated with interview requests, UK representatives' reluctance,

---

[28]We emphasise "perception" of various statuses because it is interviewees' perception more so than the researcher's "actual" status that, at least initially, is most influential for interactions. Ocampo (2012), for instance, writes that although he is Filipino, the Latino gay men he studied perceived him as a racial insider. He explains that even when his ethnographic study participants would learn that he was Asian many still refused to see him as an outsider. They instead "minimized our racial difference by saying things like, 'Filipinos are basically Spanish too' " (456). Ocampo acknowledges that respondents' racial perception of him as an insider meant they "granted me generous access to their public and private lives in ways they did not for individuals we encountered who were of other racial backgrounds, particularly Whites and non-Filipino Asians" (456).

suspicion, and discomfort was likely due to a complexity of factors including their perceptions of the interviewer's nationality. As someone who has an Igbo-Nigerian name and speaks with an identifiable North American accent, Dr Njaka would have been placed as "non-British," at least until her vocabulary and other indicators of insider status became apparent later during the interview.[29] Despite these instances of reticence, the difficulty helped to capture a particular group of perspectives within the larger group of mixed-race CSOs that align themselves closely with census categories for the purposes of their work.

As each of Dr Njaka's UK interviews progressed, the interviewees began to relax, elaborate more, and offer detailed information and stories unprompted. In this way, being perceived as having a different identity than one's interviewees is useful for collecting detailed data since "outsiders are assumed to be ignorant and require explanation."[30] In our cases, this was evidenced when interviewees' responses revealed their assumption that a US American researcher lacked knowledge of the UK. For instance, as discussed in Chapter 3, Smith marks "mixed-race White and Asian" on forms even though "that implies mixed-race White and Indian in this country." The "in this country" subtly reveals that he was attempting to explain the cultural specificity of the UK's norms around race to an outsider interviewer.

A related process when the interviewer was seen as a UK outsider was that interviewees would frame their answers in US terms. When Dave was discussing his time at university, for example, he said that his major was "Race and Culture" and added that it was "the closest thing you could get in England to a Black Studies course really."[31] In other words, rather than describing what a Race and Culture course entailed, Dave instead compared it to a major in the interviewer's home nation. Explanations and translations like these do not just demonstrate UK interviewees' knowledge of the US and/or their assumption of US-based researchers' ignorance of the UK, they also reveal that, despite relaxing and

---

[29]Interviewees' perception of a researcher as an outsider can be disrupted when insider knowledge is communicated via word choice. For example, Panfil (2017) discusses how the Black and Latino gay gang members she interviewed were "surprised" but "ultimately delighted" when she, a White lesbian, correctly used gang/criminal justice system slang and asked follow-up questions that displayed intimate knowledge of gay culture. The reverse, language revealing one's outsider status, has also been documented. During her research comparing interracial couples in the US and Brazil, for instance, Osuji (2016: 134) writes that "as a dark-skinned Black woman sporting short dreadlocks" she could "blend in as Brazilian ... as long as I did not speak." She found that this resulted in people in Brazil initially perceiving her as a national insider until they heard her non-Brazilian accented Portuguese and/or she explicitly disavowed them of the notion by stating her race/ethnicity and/or nationality.
[30]Vasquez-Tokos 2017: 2.
[31]At the time of Dave's interview in 2011, the UK had not yet developed Black Studies as a university program. In 2017, the first Black Studies program began at Birmingham City University.

speaking freely, the interviewer's perceived positionality as an outsider was always in the forefront of their minds.

The accounts that come from interviewees explaining and comparing for an outsider interviewer are beneficial in that they provide rich insights into the social construction and popular understandings of phenomena in that context. Had interviewees not offered this pre-emptively, a qualitative researcher could elicit it by asking speculative questions such as whether the interviewee has had similar or different experiences when they were in different locations such as whilst travelling.

On the other hand, though, referencing, and/or making assumptions about other contexts in order to contextualise the situation at home is frequently done uncritically.[32] This tendency was noticeable given that Dr Sims' UK interviewees drew on the same US/UK differences, and often phrased them in the same way. For example, this and other research does indicate that the norm of hypodescent is stronger in the US than the UK; however, when interviewees such as Dean and Dave refer to the "strong" US one-drop rule versus the "weak" racialisation in the UK, it risks reifying the nuanced processes of both places. Making the US and UK into oversimplified foils of one another obscures actual experiences such as Black mixed-race people in the UK being called anti-Black racial slurs and Black mixed-race people in the US being racialised as non-Black.[33] Thus, when interviewees utilise characteristics of other nations to explain aspects of their own, in order to benefit from these comparative and relational accounts cross-national qualitative researchers should gently probe further. For instance, asking if they are speaking from personal experience in different places (as Dean was) or if they are drawing on media or other general discourse they have heard (as Dave was) can illuminate even more about the phenomenon in both places.

"Well, You Know": Processes, Challenges, and Benefits of Insider Status

Perceived insider status also creates a unique set of processes and challenges that must be navigated in order to obtain comparable data. As has been noted by other qualitative researchers,[34] being seen as an insider is often associated with easier access, rapport, and intimate data collection. For example, one US census civil service employee interviewed by Dr Njaka was warm, forthcoming, and eager to share her reports, research, ideas, and opinions. In fact, this representative offered her publications that were not yet released to the public; and even after the interview she remained in contact by sending relevant updates. Furthermore, this representative provided the contact details for other mixed-race CSOs in the US that Dr Njaka could query for potential interviews. This particular employee not only worked for the Census Bureau, but also had long-standing personal interests in the campaigns for a multiracial category. A sense of shared nationality and

---

[32]Small 1994.

[33]Sims et al., under review.

[34]For example, Ocampo 2012; Panfil 2017; Vasquez-Tokos 2017.

mutual interest for research on census classification made for an easy interview process and useful information for follow-up data sources, which ultimately led to improved data quality.

In order to obtain the full benefits of easy and useful information when one has insider status, though, we had to avoid two main pitfalls. First, on the interviewees' side, assumed similarity may lead interviewees to provide overly summary information. Some of Dr Sims' US interviewees, for example, would begin to explain a point and then say "well, you know" or trail off with "and blah blah blah" and not complete what they were saying. As Dr Sims was a fellow US American who is racialised in a similar manner as them, these interviewees' assumption that she shared their experiences, whilst correct, meant that they did not initially offer the same level of detail about those experiences as UK interviewees. To obtain comparable quality data from different contexts, a researcher must probe and sometimes explicitly encourage similarly situated interviewees to "spell it out for the record."

Secondly, it is also important to remember to ask follow-up questions and probe when it is the interviewer who feels like an insider vis-à-vis interviewees. For Dr Sims' interviews with Black mixed-race women, this involved learning to suppress the impulse to respond with conversational norms of reciprocal sharing. For example, as discussed in Chapter 6, Tia's oldest daughter was told by another child "What happened to you?" in reference to her short, tightly coiled hair being different from her mother's (Tia's) long, loosely curled hair. Having been that child whose hair others compared and devalued in relation to her mother's hair, Dr Sims' first impulse was to affirm to Tia that her response to her daughter was important and loving. In addition, whilst methodologically interviews are tools to collect data about the interviewee, feminist researchers remind us to attempt to equalise power imbalances by choosing to share some information about ourselves, rather than unilaterally extract private information from others for professional gain. To accomplish both aims, when Tia finished her story Dr Sims said "Remind me to tell you about [how] I had that same thing happen to me;" and then upon completion of the interview, they discussed the topic conversationally. Structuring insider conversations at the end of the interview is thus one way to avoid the danger of straying too far off topic of the research questions whilst still sharing and benefiting from the intimate details on the topic that one can discuss when similarly situated to one's interviewees.

"Academics Are Often the Worst": Cross-National Qualitative Researchers as Homo Academicus

Though insider/outsider status regarding nationality and race/ethnicity are at the fore of cross-national qualitative research on mixed-race people, Bourdieu reminds us that as academics we are also members of a distinct social field that has its own distinct logics and practices.[35] When interviewees share the researcher's status as an academic, it can influence the type of data collected. For example,

---

[35]Bourdieu 1988[1984].

given the academy's norm of citing sources and drawing on theoretical concepts to explain phenomena, several of Dr Sims' academic interviewees referenced books they had read or used analytical concepts from their discipline when describing their experiences. Dave and Mary, both postgraduate educated, discussed specific books they had read on mixed-race identity during their interviews. John and Aaliyah, both social science postgraduate students at the time of their interviews, discussed "what are you" questions as identity invalidation and microaggressions, respectively. These offerings can lead a researcher to new and useful relevant literatures, which is especially beneficial in cross-national research since staying abreast of multiple nations' literature on a topic can be daunting. Nevertheless, because academics are habituated to particular categories of thought, concepts to use, and problems on which to focus,[36] when we interviewed a fellow academic we had to remember to consider book citations and analytical concepts firstly as data to be explored, for example, via asking what about the book or concept most resonates with the interviewee's lived experience.

By contrast, outside of studies specifically on academics, one is likely to be an outsider in this area vis-à-vis the majority, or all, of one's interviewees. Some non-academics are excited to be a research participant, as were two of Dr Sims' interviewees who said, "I hope I've been helpful" and the many who expressed thanks for the work or being able to be a part of it. Others, however, such as Dr Njaka's US-based interviewee Graeme, view academics very critically. Graeme was explicitly suspicious about Dr Njaka being an academic generally and a sociologist specifically. He critiqued some of the interview questions as being "myopic," blamed sociology as a discipline for the focus on race in societies, and criticised academia for censoring research. In comparing new media platforms to disseminate research to peer reviewed publications, he explained the following:

> We're available on – through – the internet, and let me tell you – I've written about this – probably the best thing that has ever happened to the multiracial community in the world has been the internet because all of the gatekeepers who said, "You can't do this, you can't do this," are not there anymore ....

Not only does he believe that the academy is unfavourable because of its restrictions on publication, but he went further to express his disdain for academia more broadly:

> It's because of [US] American education .... Because it's not important to them, the only country that matters is the United States, so why do we need to know anything about anything else? And that's the same with race and everything else. [...] But that's – that's the way it is and it's particularly, um, difficult to understand when it comes from academia because the academics are often the

---

[36]Bourdieu 1988[1984]: xii.

worst. And of course it's ridiculous when it comes from diversity experts; then it becomes just really stupid. [...] Yeah, we need to get outside of our little myopics [*sic*.]: "America is the only way."

Graeme believes that there are problems with the perspectives and orientations coming from a US academic system. It is likely that his impassioned perspective influenced his presumptions of Dr Njaka throughout the interview process because of his knowledge and assumptions of her status as a US American studying race and "diversity." Nevertheless, his willingness to participate in the interview and his bluntness with his perspectives made for a rich interview that provided a uniquely sceptical set of data.

Graeme's position illustrates an uneasy relationship between the academy and CSOs. This dis-ease likely influenced Dr Njaka's access to some organisations, which may have in turn affected the types of organisations that were willing to participate in the research. Additionally, this highlights their awareness of some of the academic work on mixed-race and suggests disagreement with it. This is important for academics to address because the disconnect between CSOs and the ways they are represented in academic work may hinder how useful and applicable the latter is in addressing social reality.

Conclusion: Conducting Qualitative Research in Two Countries

Whilst the US and UK were the nations of focus in our research, the processes, challenges, and benefits that we describe herein can apply to cross-cultural research in other national contexts. For example, whether due to weariness at being inundated with research requests or due to reluctance to work with those perceived from first call or e-mail as outsiders, recruiting participants to cross-national studies is often the first challenge. During cross-national data collection, the types of responses one may receive from interviewees – reserved, frank, understated, detailed – stem from the omnipresence of nationality and other social categories. Being reflexive and adaptive allows a researcher to capitalise on the benefits of both insider and outsider positionality whilst trying to avoid the pitfalls.

Regarding cross-national analytical processes, taking a joint comparative and relational approach is efficacious when considering any two nations, cultures, time-periods, or groups. Likewise, taking a multifaceted approach, for example, by analysing both the macro- and micro-level as we have herein, is useful for capturing both structure and agency. Cross-National collaborative research in which data are merged and jointly presented in one book or article[37] is one way to accomplish both. In sum, conducting focussed research on two specific nations provides unparalleled insight into the past, the present, and the future of socially constructed phenomena.

---

[37]See Sims and Joseph-Salisbury (2019) for a discussion of limitations and benefits of cross-national collaborative research involving merging independently collected data.

References

Alexander, Michelle. 2012. *The New Jim Crow: Mass Incarceration in the Age of Colorblindness*. New York, NY: The New Press.

Ali, Suki. 2003. *Mixed Race Post Race*. Oxford: BERG.

Alibhai-Brown, Yasmin. 2001. *Mixed Feelings: The Complex Lives of Mixed Race Britons*. London: The Women's Press Ltd.

Anderson, Benedict. 1991. *Imagined Communities: Reflections on the Origin and Spread of Nationalism*. London: Verso.

Anderson, Elijah. 2004. "The Cosmopolitan Canopy." *Annals of the American Academy of Political and Social Science* 595: 14–31.

Anderson, Elijah. 2011. *The Cosmopolitan Canopy: Race and Civility in Everyday Life*. New York, NY: W.W. Norton & Company.

Anzaldúa, Gloria. 1987. *Borderlands/La Frontera: The New Mestiza*. San Francisco, CA: Aunt Lute Books.

Aspinall, Peter J. and Miri Song. 2013. *Mixed Race Identities*. Basingstoke: Palgrave Macmillan.

Ballard, Roger. 1996. "Negotiating Race and Ethnicity: Exploring the Implications of the 1991 Census." *Patterns of Prejudice* 30(3): 3–33.

Banton, Michael. 1998. *Racial Theories*. Second edition. Cambridge: Cambridge University Press.

BBC News. 2019. "Danny Baker 'So, So Sorry' for Disastrous Tweet." 10 May. Retrieved 27 May 2019 (https://www.bbc.com/news/entertainment-arts-48226247).

Berger, Joseph, Bernard P. Cohen, and Morris Zelditch, Jr. 1972. "Status characteristics and social interaction." *American Sociological Review* 37(3): 241–255.

Boerman, Tessa and Samuel Reiziger. 2004. *A Knock Out*. Film. Women Make Moves.

Bonilla-Silva, Eduardo. 2018[2003]. *Racism Without Racists: Color-Blind Racism and Racial Inequality in Contemporary America*. Fifth edition. Lanham, MD: Rowman & Littlefield.

Booth, Robert. 2012. "Census 2011 Data on Religion Reveals Jedi Knights are in Decline." *The Guardian*. 11 December. Retrieved 13 May 2019 (https://www.theguardian.com/uk/2012/dec/11/census-data-religion-jedi-knights).

Bourdieu, Pierre. 1988[1984]. *Homo Academicus*. Palo Alto, CA: Stanford University Press.

Bradford, Ben. 2006. "Who Are the 'Mixed' Ethnic Group?" *Social and Welfare*. London: Office for National Statistics.

Bradshaw, Carla K. 1992. "Beauty and the Beast: On Racial Ambiguity." Pp. 77–88 in *Racially mixed people in America*, edited by M. P. P. Root. Newbury Park, CA: Sage Publications.

Bratter, Jenifer. 2007. "Will 'Multiracial' Survive to the Next Generation? The Racial Classification of Children of Multiracial Parents." *Social Forces* 86(2): 821–849.

Brunsma, David L. and Kerry Ann Rockquemore. 2001. "The New Color Complex: Appearances and Biracial Identity." *Identity* 3(1): 29–52.

Brunsma, David L. 2006. "Public Categories, Private Identities: Exploring Regional Differences in the Biracial Experience." *Social Science Research* 35(3): 555–576.

Buggs, Shantel. 2017a. "Does (Mixed-)Race Matter? The Role of Race in Interracial Sex, Dating, and Marriage." *Sociology Compass* 11: 1–13; e12531.

Buggs, Shantel. 2017b. "Dating in the Time of #BlackLivesMatter: Exploring Mixed-Race Women's Discourses of Race and Racism." *Sociology of Race and Ethnicity* 3(4): 538–551.

Buggs, Shantel. 2019. "Color, Culture, or Cousin? Multiracial Americans and Framing Boundaries in Interracial Relationships." *Journal of Marriage of Family* 81(5): 1221–1236. https://doi.org/10.1111/jomf.12583

Bullock, Jungmiwha Suk. 2010. *Multiracial Politics or the Politics of Being Multiracial? Racial Theory, Civic Engagement, and Socio-political Participation in a Contemporary Society*. PhD Thesis. Los Angeles, CA: University of Southern California.

Burke, Peter J. and Jan E. Stets. 2009. *Identity Theory*. Oxford: Oxford University Press

Butler, Judith. 1990. *Gender Trouble and the Subversion of Identity*. London: Routledge.

Caballero, Chamion. 2004. '*Mixed Race Projects': Perceptions, Constructions and Implications of Mixed Race in the UK and USA*. PhD Thesis. Bristol: University of Bristol.

Campbell, Mary E. and Lisa Troyer. 2007. "The Implications of Racial Misclassification by Observers." *American Sociological Review* 72(5): 750–765.

Candelario, Ginetta. 2010. *Black Behind the Ears: Dominican Racial Identity from Museums to Beauty Shops*. Chapel Hill, NC: Duke University Press.

Cazenave, Noel. 2015. *Conceptualizing Racism: Breaking the Chains of Racially Accommodative Language*. Lanham, MD: Rowman & Littlefield.

Charmaz, Kathy. 2006. *Constructing Grounded Theory: A Practical Guide Through Qualitative Analysis*. Los Angeles, CA: Sage.

Choldin, Harvey. 1994. *Looking for the Last Percent: The Controversy Over Census Undercounts*. New Brunswick, NJ: Rutgers University Press.

Clements, Ben. 2017. "Attitudes Towards Gay Rights." British Religion in Numbers. January 2017. Retrieved 23 May 2019 (http://www.brin.ac.uk/figures/attitudes-towards-gay-rights).

Cohen, Jean L. 1985. "Strategy or Identity: New Theoretical Paradigms and Contemporary Social Movements." *Social Research* 52(4): 663–716.

Cohn, D'vera. 2017. "Seeking Better Data on Hispanics, Census Bureau May Change How it Asks About Race." *Fact Tank: News in the Numbers*. Pew Research Center. 20 April. Retrieved 1 April 2019 (https://www.pewresearch.org/fact-tank/2017/04/20/seeking-better-data-on-hispanics-census-bureau-may-change-how-it-asks-about-race).

Collins, Patrice Hill. 2004. *Black Sexual Polices: African Americans, Gender, and the New Racism*. New York, NY: Routledge.

Crenshaw, Kimberle. 1989. "Demarginalizing the Intersection of Race and Sex: A Black Feminist Critique of Antidiscrimination Doctrine, Feminist Theory and Antiracist Politics." *University of Chicago Legal Forum* 1989(1): 139–167.

Currington, Celeste Vaughan, Ken-Hou Lin, and Jennifer Hickes Lundquist. 2015. "Positioning Multiraciality in Cyberspace: Treatment of Multiracial Daters in an Online Dating Website." *American Sociological Review* 80(4): 764–788.

Dabiri, Emma. 2019. *Don't Touch My Hair*. London: Penguin Random House.

DaCosta, Kimberly McClain. 2007. *Making Multiracials: State, Family, and Market in the Redrawing of the Color Line*. Stanford, CA: Stanford University Press.

Daniel, G. Reginald. 2006. *Race and Multiraciality in Brazil and the United States: Converging Paths?* University Park, PA: Pennsylvania State University Press.

Daniel, G. Reginald, Laura Kina, Wei Ming Dariotis, and Camilla Fojas. 2014. "Emerging Paradigms in Critical Mixed Race Studies." *Journal of Critical Mixed Race Studies* 1(1): 6–65.

Davenport, Lauren. 2018. *Politics Beyond Black and White: Biracial Identity and Attitudes in America*. Cambridge: Cambridge University Press.

Denscombe, Martyn. 2007. *The Good Research Guide*. Third edition. Maidenhead: Open University Press.

Desmond, Matthew and Mustafa Emirbayer. 2016[2010]. *Race in America*. New York, NY: Norton.

Deterding, Nicole and Mary Waters. 2018. "Flexible Coding of In-depth Interviews: A Twenty-first-century Approach." *Sociological Methods & Research*. doi: 10.1177/0049124118799377.

Devos, Thierry and Mahzarin R. Banaji. 2005. "American = White?" *Journal of Personality and Social Psychology* 88(3): 447–466.

DiAngelo, Robin. 2018. *White Fragility: Why It's So Hard for White People to Talk About Racism*. Boston, MA: Beacon Press.

Dikötter, Frank. 2008. "The Racialization of the Globe: An Interactive Interpretation." *Ethnic and Racial Studies* 31(8): 1478–1496.

Dover, Cedric. 1937. *Half-Caste*. London: Secker & Warburg.

Drake, Bruce. 2013. "How LGBT Adults See Society and How the Public Sees Them." *Pew Research Center*. 25 June. Retrieved 23 May 2019 (https://www.pewresearch.org/fact-tank/2013/06/25/how-lgbt-adults-see-society-and-how-the-public-sees-them/).

Du Bois W. E. B. 1903. *The Souls of Black Folk*. Chicago, IL: A. C. McClurg and Company.

Dumbrell, John. 2009. "The US–UK Special Relationship: Taking the 21st-Century Temperature." *The British Journal of Politics and International Relations* 11: 64–78.

Eberhardt, Jennifer L., Paul G. Davies, Valerie J. Purdie-Vaughns, and Sheri Lynn Johnson. 2006. "Looking Deathworthy: Perceived Stereotypicality of Black Defendants Predicts Capital-Sentencing Outcomes." *Psychological Science* 17(5): 383–386.

Edwards, Rosalind, Suki Ali, Chamion Caballero, and Miri Song, eds. 2012. *International Perspectives on Racial and Ethnic Mixedness and Mixing*. Oxfordshire: Routledge.

Elam, Michele. 2011. *The Souls of Mixed Folk: Race, Politics, and Aesthetics in the New Millennium*. Stanford, CA: Stanford University Press.

Essed, Philomena. 1991. *Understanding Everyday Racism*. London: SAGE Publications.

Essed, Philomena and David Theo Goldberg, eds. 2002. *Race Critical Theories: Text and Context*. Malden, MA: Blackwell Publishers Inc.

Evens-Winters, Venus E. 2019. *Black Feminism in Qualitative Inquiry: A Mosaic for Writing Our Daughter's Body*. New York, NY: Routledge.

Fairclough, Norman. 2010. *Critical Discourse Analysis: The Critical Study of Language*. Second edition. Harlow: Pearson Education Limited.

Fanon, Frantz. 1961. *The Wretched of the Earth*. New York, NY: Grove Press.

Fanon, Frantz. 1967. *Black Skins, White Masks*. New York, NY: Grove Press.

Foucault, Michel. 1972. "The Discourse on Language." Pp. 215–237 in *The Archaeology of Knowledge (L'ordre du Discourse)*, edited by M. Foucault. New York, NY: Harper Colophon.

Foucault, Michel. 1978. *The History of Sexuality, Volume I: An Introduction*. New York, NY: Pantheon Books.

Freeman, Jonathan B., Andrew M. Penner, Aliya Saperstein, Matthias Scheutz, and Nalini Ambady. 2011. "Looking the Part: Social Status Cues Shape Race Perception." *PLoS ONE* 6(9): e25107.

Gans, Herbert J. 1979. "Symbolic Ethnicity: The Future of Ethnic Groups and Cultures in America." *Ethnic and Racial Studies* 2(1): 1–19.

Garfinkel, Harold. 1967. *Studies in Ethnomethodology*. Cambridge: Polity Press.

Garner, Steve. 2010. *Racisms: An Introduction*. London: SAGE Publications.

Gates, Henry Louis, Jr. 2014. "High Cheekbones and Straight Black Hair? 100 Amazing Facts About the Negro: Why Most Black People Aren't 'Part Indian,' Despite Family Lore." *The Root*. 29 December. Retrieved 1 June 2019 (https://www.theroot.com/high-cheekbones-and-straight-black-hair-1790878167).

Gibson, Campbell and Jung Kay. 2002. "Historical Census Statistics on Population Totals By Race, 1790 to 1990, and By Hispanic Origin, 1970 to 1990, For The United States, Regions, Divisions, and States." *Population Division: Working Paper No. 56*. Washington, DC: United States Census Bureau.

Gil, Laruen. 2017. "Meghan Markle 'Won't be Allowed to be Black Princess' by Royal Family, Experts Say." *Newsweek*. 27 November. Retrieved 28 November 2017 (http://www.newsweek.com/meghan-markle-will-be-told-royal-teachers-hide-her-biracial-identity-wont-be-723737).

Gilchrist, Eletra S. and Ronald S. Jackson II. 2012. "Articulating the Heuristic Value of African-American Communication Studies." *Review of Communication* 12(3): 1–14.

Gillett, Francesca. 2019. "Archie Harrison: The Meaning Behind the Royal Baby's Name." *BBC News*. 8 May. Retrieved 10 July 2019 (https://www.bbc.co.uk/news/uk-48204592).

Glaser, Barney G. and Anselm L. Strauss. 1967. *The Discovery of Grounded Theory: Strategies for Qualitative Research*. New Brunswick, NJ: Transaction.

Glasgow, Joshua. 2009. *A Theory of Race*. New York City, NY: Routledge.

Gobineau, Joseph Arthur, Comte de. 2004. "Recapitulation: The Respective Characteristics of the Three Great Races; The Superiority of the White Type, and, Within This Type, of the Aryan Fam." Pp. 39–41 in *"Mixed Race" Studies: A Reader,* edited by J. Ifekwunigwe. London: Routledge.

Goffman, Erving. 1967. *Interaction Ritual.* New York, NY: Doubleday/Anchor.

Goffman, Erving. 1971. *Relations in Public: Microstudies of the Public Order*. New York, NY: Basic Books.

Goldberg, David Theo. 1995. "Made in the USA." Pp. 237–257 in *American Mixed Race: The Culture of Microdiversity,* edited by N. Zack. Lanham, MD: Rowman & Littlefield Publishers, Inc.

Goldberg, David Theo. 2009. "Racial Comparisons, Relational Racisms: Some Thoughts on Method." *Ethnic and Racial Studies* 32(7): 1271–1282.

Goldberg, David Theo. 2015. *Are We All Post Racial Yet? Debating Race*. Cambridge: Polity Press.

Gordon, Lewis R. 1995. "Critical 'Mixed Race'?" *Social Identities: Journal for the Study of Race, Nation and Culture* 1(2): 381–395.

Graves, Joseph L., Jr. 2001. *The Emperor's New Clothes: Biological Theories of Race at the Millennium*. New Brunswick, NJ: Rutgers University Press.

Greenfield, Patrick and Nadeem Badshah. 2019. "Police to Investigate Danny Baker Over Royal Baby Tweet." *The Guardian*. 10 May. Retrieved 27 May 2019 (https://www.theguardian.com/media/2019/may/10/police-investigate-danny-baker-royal-baby-chimpanzee-tweet).

Greenspan, Rachel E. 2019. "Royal Baby Archie Has a Different Last Name Than His Father, Prince Harry. Here's Why." *Time*. 8 May. Retrieved 10 July 2019 (https://time.com/5571788/meghan-markle-royal-baby-last-name).

Grieco, Elizabeth M. and Rachel C. Cassidy. 2001. "Overview of Race and Hispanic Origin." *Census 2000 Brief*. Washington, DC: US Department of Commerce.

Gov.uk. 2019. "National Statistics. Fostering in England 2017 to 2018: Main Findings." 31 January. Retrieved 1 June 2019 (https://www.gov.uk/government/publications/fostering-in-england-1-april-2017-to-31-march-2018/fostering-in-england-2017-to-2018-main-findings).

Hainer, Peter C. 1987. *A Brief and Qualitative Anthropological Study Exploring the Reasons for Census Coverage Error Among Low Income Black Households*. Washington, DC: U.S. Bureau of the Census, Center for Survey Methods Research.

Hanson, F. Allan. 2001. "Donor Insemination: Eugenic and Feminist Implications." *Medical Anthropology Quarterly* 15(3): 287–311.

Hernández-Campoy, Juan and Juan Camillo Conde-Silvestre. 2012. *Handbook of Historical Sociolinguistics*. Oxford: Wiley-Blackwell.

Hernández, Tanya Katerí. 2018. *Multiracial and Civil Rights: Mixed-Race Stories of Discrimination*. New York, NY: New York University Press.

Herring, Cedric. 2004. "Skin Deep: Race and Complexion in the 'Color-Blind' Era." Pp. 1–21 in *Skin Deep: How Race and Complexion Matter in the 'Color-Blind' Era,* edited by C. Herring, V. M. Keith, and H. D. Horton. Chicago, IL: University of Illinois Press.

Hirsch, Lily, Kirrilly Thompson, and Danielle Every. 2014. "From Computer to Commuter: Considerations for the Use of Social Networking Sites for Participant Recruitment." *The Qualitative Report* 19(2): 1–13.

HM Government. 2018. *Help Shape Our Future: The 2021 Census of Population and Housing in England and Wales.* London: Crown.

Hochschild, Jennifer. 2007. Personal Communication. June 2007.

Hochschild, Jennifer, Vesla Weaver, and Traci Burch. 2012. *Creating a New Racial Order: How Immigration, Multiracialisms, Genomics, and the Young Can Remake Race in America.* Princeton, NJ: Princeton University Press.

Holiday, Nicole. 2019. "When "Mixed" Isn't Enough." 28 May. Retrieved 28 May 2019 (https://www.dictionary.com/e/when-mixed-isnt-enough/).

Hordge-Freeman, Elizabeth. 2015. *The Color of Love: Racial Features, Stigma and Socialization in Black Brazilian Families.* Austin, TX: University of Texas Press.

HoSang, Daniel Martinez and Oneka LaBennett. 2012. "Introduction." Pp. 1–17 in *Racial Formation in the Twenty-first Century,* edited by D. M. HoSang, O. LaBennett, and L. Pulido. Berkeley, CA: University of California Press.

Humes, Karen, Nicolas A. Jones, and Roberto R. Ramirez. 2011. "Overview of Race and Hispanic Origin: 2010." *Census 2010 Brief.* Washington, DC: US Department of Commerce.

Ifekwunigwe, Jayne O., ed. 2004. *'Mixed Race' Studies: A Reader.* London: Routledge.

Jivraj, Stephen. 2012. "How Has Ethnic Diversity Grown 1991-2001-2011?" *Dynamics of Diversity: Evidence from the 2011 Census.* Manchester: Centre on Dynamics of Ethnicity (CoDE).

Jones, Nicolas A. and Amy Symens Smith. 2001. "Two or More Races Population: 2000." *Census 2000 Brief.* Washington, DC: US Department of Commerce.

Jones, Nicolas A. and Jungmiwha Bullock. 2012. "The Two or More Races Population: 2010." *Census 2010 Brief.* Washington, DC: US Department of Commerce.

Joseph-Salisbury, Remi. 2018. *Black Mixed-Race Men: Transatlanticity, Hybridity and 'Post-Racial' Resilience.* Bingley: Emerald Publishing.

Joseph-Salisbury, Remi and Laura Connelly. 2018. "'If Your Hair is Relaxed, White People are Relaxed. If Your Hair is Nappy, They're Not Happy:' Black Hair as a Site of 'Post-racial' Social Control in English Schools." *Social Sciences*, 7, 219. doi:10.3390/socsci7110219

Kaw, Eugenia. 1993. "Medicalization of Racial Features: Asian American Women and Cosmetic Surgery." *Medical Anthropology Quarterly* 7(1): 74–89.

Keller, Reiner. 2013. *Doing Discourse Research: An Introduction for Social Scientists.* London: SAGE Publications.

Kertzer, David and Dominique Arel. 2002. "Census, Identity Formation, and Political Power." Pp. 1–42 in *Census and Identity: The Politics of Race, Ethnicity, and Language in National Censuses,* edited by D. Kertzer and D. Arel. Cambridge: Cambridge University Press.

Khanna, Nikki. 2004. "The Role of Reflected Appraisals in Racial Identity: The Case of Multiracial Asians." *Social Psychology Quarterly* 67: 115–131.

Khanna, Nikki. 2011. *Biracial in America: Forming and Performing Racial Identity.* Lanham, MD: Lexington Books.

Khanna, Nikki and Cathryn Johnson. 2010. "Passing as Black: Racial Identity Work among Biracial Americans." *Social Psychology Quarterly* 73(4): 380–97.

King, Alissa R. 2011. "Environmental Influences on the Development of Female College Students Who Identify as Multiracial/Biracial–Bisexual/Pansexual." *Journal of College Student Development* 52(4): 440–455.

King-O'Riain, Rebecca C., Stephen Small, Minelle Mahtani, Miri Song, and Paul Spickard, eds. 2014. *Global Mixed Race*. New York City, NY: New York University Press.

Knox, Robert. 1850. *The Races of Men: A Fragment*. Philadelphia, PA: Lea & Blanchard. Retrieved 3 December 2016 (https://archive.org/stream/racesofmenfragme00knox).

La Flamme, Michelle. 2019. *Soma Text: Living, Writing, and Staging Racial Hybridity*. Waterloo, Canada: Wilfrid Laurier University Press.

Laster Pirtle, Whitney N. 2014. "Racial Limbo: A Systematic Study of the History of Coloured South Africans and Their Contemporary Attitudes, Perceptions of Deprivation, and Racial Identifications." PhD Thesis. Nashville, TN: Vanderbilt University. (Officially accepted September – ProQuest Dissertations Publishing, 2014. 10295588.)

Leddy-Owen, Charles. 2014. "'It's True, I'm English ... I'm Not Lying': Essentialized and Precarious English Identities." *Ethnic and Racial Studies* 37(8): 1448–1466.

Lemi, Danielle. 2018. "The Multiracial Candidate (Dis)Advantage." Presented at the University of Pennsylvania Symposium on the Politics of Immigration, Race, and Ethnicity, September 21, Philadelphia, PA.

Lemi, Danielle and Nadia E. Brown. 2019. "Melanin and Curls: Evaluation of Black Women Candidates." *Journal of Race, Ethnicity, and Politics* 4(2): 259–296.

Littlejohn, Krystale E. 2019. "Race and Social Boundaries: How Multiracial Identification Matters for Intimate Relationships." *Social Currents* 6(2): 177–194.

López, Ian Haney. 2006[1996]. *White by Law: The legal Construction of Race*. New York, NY: New York University Press.

Loveman, Mara and Jeronimo Muniz. 2007. "How Puerto Rico Became White: Boundary Dynamics and Intercensus Racial Reclassification." *American Sociological Review* 72(6): 915–939.

MacLin, Otto H. and Roy S. Malpass. 2001. "Racial Categorization of Faces: The Ambiguous Race Face Effect." *Psychology, Public Policy, and Law* 7(1): 98–118.

Mahtani, Minelle. 2014. *Mixed Race Amnesia: Resisting the Romanticization of Multiraciality*. Vancouver: UBC Press.

Markus, Hazel Rose and Paula M. L. Moya, eds. 2010. *Doing Race: 21 Essays for the 21st Century*. New York, NY: W.W. Norton.

Martinez Echazabal, Lourdes. 1998. "Mestizaje and the Discourse of National/Cultural Identity in Latin America, 1845–1959." *Latin American Perspectives* 25(3): 21–42.

Marx, Anthony W. 1998. *Making Race and Nation: A Comparison of South Africa, The United States, and Brazil*. Cambridge: Cambridge University Press.

Mason, David. 1999. "The Continuing Significance of Race? Teaching Ethnic and Racial Studies in Sociology." Pp. 13–28 in *Ethnic and Racial Studies Today*, edited by M. Bulmer and J. Solomos. London: Routledge.

Mason, Jennifer. 2011. "Facet Methodology: The Case for an Inventive Research Orientation." *Methodological Innovations Online* 6(3): 75–92.

Masuoka, Natalie. 2017. *Multiracial Identity and Racial Politics in the United States*. Oxford: Oxford University Press.

McAdam, Doug, John D. McCarthy, and Mayer N. Zald, eds. 1996. *Comparative Perspectives on Social Movements: Political Opportunities, Mobilizing Structures, and Cultural Framings*. Cambridge: Cambridge University Press.

McKinnon, Jesse. 2001. "The Black Population: 2000." *Census 2000 Brief*. Washington, DC: US Department of Commerce.

Mills, Melinda. 2017. *The Borders of Race: Patrolling "Multiracial" Identities*. Boulder, CO: First Forum Press.

Mirza, Heidi Safia. 2015. "'Harvesting Our Collective Intelligence': Black British Feminism in Post-Race Times." *Women's Studies International Forum* 51: 1–9.

Mitchell, Valory and Robert-Jay Green. 2007. "Different Storks for Different Folks." *Journal of GLBT Family Studies* 3(2–3): 81–104.

Monk, Ellis. 2014. "Skin Tone Stratification among Black Americans, 2001–2003." *Social Forces* 92(4): 1313–1337.

Monk, Ellis. 2015. "The Cost of Color: Skin Color, Discrimination, and Health among African-Americans." *American Journal of Sociology* 121(2): 396–444.

Monk, Ellis. 2019. "The Color of Punishment: African Americans, Skin Tone, and the Criminal Justice System." *Ethnic and Racial Studies* 42(10): 1593–1612. doi:10.1080 /01419870.2018.1508736.

Moraga, Cherríe. 2015[1979]. "La Güera." Pp. 22–29 in *This Bridge Called My Back, Fourth Edition: Writings by Radical Women of Color,* edited by C. Moraga and G. Andalúza. Albany, NY: State University of New York Press.

Morning, Ann. 2008. "Ethnic Classification in Global Perspective: A Cross-National Survey of the 2000 Census Round." *Population Research and Policy Review* 27(2): 239–272.

Mullings, Leith. 1997. *On Our Own Terms. Race, Class, and Gender in the Lives of African American Women.* New York, NY: Routledge.

Murji, Karim and John Solomos. 2005. "Introduction: Racialization in Theory and Practice." Pp. 1–27 in *Racialization: Studies in Theory and Practice,* edited by K. Murji and J. Solomos. Oxford: Oxford University Press.

Neblett, Touré. 2011. *Who's Afraid of Post-Blackness?: What it Means to Be Black Now.* New York, NY: Free Press.

Newman, Alyssa. 2019. "Desiring the Standard Light Skin: Black Multiracial Boys, Masculinity and Exotification." *Identities* 26(1): 107–125.

Newsround. 2019. "Royal Baby Harry and Meghan Name Baby Son Archie Harrison." *BBC.* 8 May. Retrieved 10 July 2019 (https://www.bbc.co.uk/newsround/48204168).

Nittle, Nadra. 2017. "It's Time to Stop Hair-Policing Children of Color." *Racked.* 25 May. Retrieved 9 July 2018 (https://www.racked.com/2017/5/25/15685456/hair-policing-schools-braids-afros).

Njaka, Chinelo L. 2013a. "Mixed-Race Americans." Pp. 1477–1481 in *Multicultural America: A Multimedia Encyclopedia,* edited by C. E. Cortés. Thousand Oaks, CA: SAGE Publications, Inc.

Njaka, Chinelo L. 2013b. "Regional Patterns." Pp. 78–82 in *Multicultural America: A Multimedia Encyclopedia,* edited by C. E. Cortés. Thousand Oaks, CA: SAGE Publications, Inc.

Nobles, Melissa. 2000. *Shades of Citizenship: Race and the Census in Modern Politics.* Stanford, CA: Stanford University Press.

Nobles, Melissa. 2002. "Racial Categorization and Censuses." Pp. 43–70 in *Census and Identity: The Politics of Race, Ethnicity, and Language in National Censuses,* edited by D. Kertzer and D. Arel. Cambridge: Cambridge University Press.

Nordqvist, Petra. 2010. "Out of Sight, Out of Mind: Family Resemblances in Lesbian Donor Conception." *Sociology* 44(6): 1128–1144.

Ocampo, Anthony C. 2012. "Making masculinity: Negotiations of gender presentation among Latino gay men." *Latino Studies* 10(4): 448–472.

Office for National Statistics (ONS). 2003. "Quality of Data Capture and Coding: Evaluation Report." *Census 2001 Review and Evaluation.* London: Office for National Statistics.

Office for National Statistics (ONS). 2012a. "2011-2001 Census in England and Wales Questionnaire Comparability." *2011 Census: User Guide.* London: Office for National Statistics.

Office for National Statistics (ONS). 2012b. "Ethnicity and National Identity in England and Wales 2011." 11 December. Retrieved 22 June 2014 (http://www.ons.gov.uk/ons/dcp171776_290558.pdf).

Office for National Statistics (ONS). 2015. "Ethnic Group." *Harmonised Concepts and Questions for Social Data Sources.* Version 3.3. London: Office for National Statistics.

Office for National Statistics (ONS). 2018. "Census." 3 October. Retrieved 12 February 2019 (https://www.ons.gov.uk/census).

Office of Management and Budget (OMB). 1997. *Revisions to the Standards for the Classification of Federal Data on Race.* Washington, DC: Office of Management and Budget.

Olumide, Jill. 2002. *Raiding the Gene Pool: The Social Construction of Mixed Race.* London: Pluto Press.

Omi, Michael and Howard Winant. 1994. *Racial Formation in the United States from the 1960s to the 1990s.* New York, NY: Routledge.

Omi, Michael and Howard Winant. 2015. *Racial Formation in the United States.* Third edition. New York City, NY: Routledge.

Opie, Tina R., and Katherine W. Phillips. 2015. "Hair Penalties: The Negative Influence of Afrocentric Hair on Ratings of Black Women's Dominance and Professionalism." *Frontiers in Psychology* 6(131): 1–14.

Osuji, Chinyere. 2016. "An African/Nigerian-American Studying Black-White Couples in Los Angeles and Rio de Janeiro." Pp. 123–138 in *Race and the Politics of Knowledge Production: Diaspora and Black Transnational Scholarship in the United States and Brazil,* edited by G. L. Mitchell-Walthour and E. Hordge-Freeman. Basingstoke: Palgrave Macmillan.

Osuji, Chinyere. 2019. *Boundaries of Love: Interracial Marriage and the Meaning of Race in the United States and Brazil.* New York, NY: New York University Press.

Owen, Charlie. 2001. "'Mixed Race' in Official Statistics." Pp. 134–153 in *Rethinking 'Mixed Race,'* edited by D. Parker and M. Song. London: Pluto Press.

Panfil, Vanessa R. 2017. *The Gang's All Queer: The Lives of Gay Gang Members.* New York, NY: New York University Press.

Paragg, Jillian. 2017. "'What are you?': Mixed race responses to the racial gaze." *Ethnicities* 17(3): 277–298.

Parker, David and Miri Song. 2001. "Introduction: Rethinking 'Mixed Race.' " Pp. 1–22 in *Rethinking 'Mixed Race,'* edited by D. Parker and M. Song. London: Pluto Press.

Pascoe, C. J. 2011. *Dude, You're a Fag: Masculinity and Sexuality in High School* (2nd edition). Berkeley, CA: University of California Press.

Perlmann, Joel and Mary C. Waters, eds. 2002. *The New Race Question: How the Census Counts Multiracial Individuals.* New York, NY: Russell Sage Foundation.

Petter, Olivia. 2019. "Royal Baby Christening: Couple's Decision to Keep Celebration Private Sparks Criticism." *Independent.* 6 July. Retrieved 10 July 2019 (https://www.independent.co.uk/life-style/archie-christening-royal-baby-criticism-private-cere-mony-windsor-castle-criticism-twitter-a8991326.html).

Pew Research Center. 2015. *Multiracial in America: Proud, Diverse and Growing in Numbers.* Washington, DC: Pew Charitable Trusts.

Polkinghorne, Donald E. 1995. "Narrative Configuration in Qualitative Analysis." *International Journal of Qualitative Studies in Education* 8(1): 5–23.

Prewitt, Kenneth. 2000. "The US Decennial Census: Political Questions, Scientific Answers." *Population and Development Review* 26(1): 1–16.

Rallu, Jean-Louis, Victor Piché, and Patrick Simon. 2004. "Demography and Ethnicity: An Ambiguous Relationship." Pp. 531–549 in *Demography: Analysis and Synthesis. A Treatise in Population Studies, Volume 3,* edited by G. Caselli, J. Vallin, and G. Wunsch. Amsterdam, NL/Oxford: Elsevier/Academic Press.

Rastogi, Sonya, Tallese D. Johnson, Elizabeth M. Hoeffel, and Malcolm P. Drewery, Jr. 2011. "The Black Population: 2010." *Census 2010 Brief.* Washington, DC: US Department of Commerce.

Relethford, John H. 1996. *Fundamentals of Biological Anthropology.* New York City, NY: McGraw-Hill.

Relethford, John H. 2009. "Race and Global Patterns of Phenotypic Variation." *American Journal of Physical Anthropology* 139(1): 16–22.

Remedios, Jessica D. and Alison L. Chasteen. 2013. "Finally, Someone Who "Gets" Me! Multiracial People Value Others' Accuracy About Their Race" *Cultural Diversity and Ethnic Minority Psychology* 19(4): 453–460.

Rendall, Michael. 2005. "Focus on: Ethnicity & Identity." *National Statistics*. London: Office for National Statistics.

Reuters. 2019. "Census 2020: Justice Department Brings in New Team to Fight for Citizenship Question." *The Guardian*. 8 July. Retrieved 10 July 2019 (https://www.theguardian.com/us-news/2019/jul/08/census-2020-justice-department-brings-in-new-team-to-fight-for-citizenship-question).

Ritchie, Jane and Jane Lewis, eds. 2003. *Qualitative Research Practice: A Guide for Social Science Students and Researchers*. London: SAGE Publications.

Robinson, Brandon Andrew. 2016. "'Personal Preference' as the New Racism: Gay Desire and Racial Cleansing in Cyberspace." *Sociology of Race and Ethnicity* 1(2): 317–330.

Rockquemore, Kerry Ann. 1999. "Between Black and White: Exploring the 'Biracial' Experience." *Race and Society* 1: 197–212.

Rockquemore, Kerry Ann and Patricia Arend. 2002. "Opting for White: Choice, Fluidity and Racial Identity Construction in Post Civil-Rights America." *Race and Society* 5: 49–64.

Rockquemore, Kerry Ann and Tracy Laszloffy. 2005. *Raising Biracial Children*. Lanham, MD: AltaMira Press.

Rodríguez, Clara E. 2000. *Changing Race: Latinos, the Census, and the History of Ethnicity in the United States*. New York City, NY: New York University Press.

Rogers, Katie. 2019. "The Painful Roots of Trump's 'Go Back' Comment." *The New York Times* 16 July.

Root, Maria P. P. 1990. "Resolving 'other' status: Identity development of biracial individuals." Pp. 185–206 in *Diversity and Complexity in Feminist Therapy*, edited by L. S. Brown and M. P. P. Root. New York, NY: Harrington Park Press.

Root, Maria P. P., ed. 1992. *Racially Mixed People in America*. Newbury Park, CA: SAGE Publications.

Root, Maria P. P. ed. 1996. *The Multiracial Experience: Racial Borders as the New Frontier.* Thousand Oaks, CA: SAGE Publications.

Roth, Wendy D. 2016. "The Multiple Dimensions of Race." *Ethnic and Racial Studies* 39(8): 1310–1338.

Roth, Wendy D. 2018. "Unsettled Identities amid Settled Classifications? Toward a Sociology of Racial Appraisals." *Ethnic and Racial Studies* 41(6): 1–20.

Russell, Kathy, Midge Wilson, and Ronals Hall. 1992. *The Color Complex: The Politics of Skin Color Among African Americans.* New York, NY: Harcourt Brace Jovanovich.

Ryan, Maura, Amanda Moras and Eve Shapiro. 2010. "Race Matters in Lesbian Donor Insemination: Whiteness and Heteronormativity as Co-Constituted Narratives." Presented at the Annual Meeting of the American Sociological Association. Abstract Retrieved 3 July 2015 (http://citation.allacademic.com/meta/p_mla_apa_research_citation/4/1/0/0/4/p410047_index.html).

Saad, Layla F. 2020. *Me and White Supremacy: How to Recognise Your Privilege, Combat Racism and Change the World.* London: Quercus Publishing.

Scott, John and Gordon Marshall, eds. 2009. *A Dictionary of Sociology*. Oxford: Oxford University Press.

Sexton, Jared. 2008. *Amalgamation Schemes: Antiblackness and the Critique of Multiracialism*. Minneapolis, MN: University of Minnesota.

Simpson, Ludi. 2003. "How Many People Live on This Island?" *Radical Statistics* 82: 13–19.

Sims, Jennifer Patrice. 2012. "Beautiful Stereotypes: The Relationship between Physical Attractiveness and Mixed Race Identity." *Identities* 19(1): 61–80.

Sims, Jennifer Patrice. 2014. *Doing Race: Physical Appearance, Identity, and the Micro-politics of Racial Ambiguity*. PhD Thesis. Madison, WI: University of Wisconsin-Madison.

Sims, Jennifer Patrice. 2016. "Reevaluation of the Influence of Appearance and Reflected Appraisals for Mixed-Race Identity: The Role of Consistent Inconsistent Racial Perception." *Sociology of Race and Ethnicity* 2(4): 569–583.

Sims, Jennifer Patrice. 2018. "'It Represents Me:' Tattooing Mixed-Race Identity." *Sociological Spectrum* 38(4): 243–255.

Sims, Jennifer Patrice and Remi Joseph-Salisbury. 2019. "'We Were All Just the Black Kids:' Black Mixed-Race Men and the Importance of Adolescent Peer Groups for Identity Development." *Social Currents* 6(1): 51–66.

Sims, Jennifer Patrice, Whitney N. Laster Pirtle, and Iris Johnson-Arnold. "Doing Hair, Doing Race: The Influence of Hairstyle on Racial Perception Across the US." (Under Review as Revise and Resubmit at *Ethnic and Racial Studies*).

Small, Stephen. 1994. *Racialised Barriers: The Black Experience in the United States and England in the 1980s*. London: Routledge.

Song, Miri. 2003. *Choosing Ethnic Identity*. Cambridge: Polity Press.

Song, Miri. 2017. *Multiracial Parents: Mixed Families, Generational Change, and the Future of Race*. New York, NY: New York University Press.

Song, Miri and Peter Aspinall. 2012. "Is Racial Mismatch a Problem for Young 'Mixed Race' People in Britain? The Findings of Qualitative Research." *Ethnicities* 12(6): 730–753.

Spencer, Rainier. 2004. "Assessing Multiracial Identity Theory and Politics: The Challenge of Hypodescent." *Ethnicities* 4(3): 357–379.

Spencer, Rainier. 2010. "Militant Multiraciality: Rejecting Race and Rejecting the Conveniences of Complicity." Pp. 155–172 in *Color Struck: Essays on Race and Ethnicity in Global Perspective,* edited by J. O. Adekunle and H. V. Williams. Lanham, MD: University Press of America.

Spencer, Rainier. 2011. *Reproducing Race: The Paradox of Generation Mix*. Boulder, CO: Lynne Rienner Publishers.

Spencer, Rainier. 2014. "'Only the News They Want to Print': Mainstream Media and Critical Mixed-Race Studies." *Journal of Critical Mixed Race Studies* 1(1): 162–182.

Spickard, Paul. 1992. "The Illogic of American Racial Categories." Pp. 12–23 in *Racially Mixed People in America,* edited by M. P. P. Root. Newbury Park, CA: SAGE Publications.

Stockstill, Casey. 2018. "Does Asserting A Non-Black Identity Elicit More Positive Evaluations? White Observers' Reactions to Black, Biracial, Multiracial, And White Job Applicants." *Sociological Perspectives* 61(1): 126–144.

Stonequist, Everett V. 1937. *Marginal Man: A Study in Personality and Culture Conflict*. New York, NY: Scribner's.

Storti, Anna. 2017. "The Case of Daniel Holtzclaw: Anti-Blackness, Transpacific Migration, and the Politics of Multiracialism." Presented at the Critical Mixed Race Studies Conference, February 24, Los Angeles, CA.

Strmic-Pawl, Hephzibah V., Brandon A. Jackson, and Steve Garner 2018. "Race Counts: Racial and Ethnic Data on the U.S. Census and the Implications for Tracking Inequality." *Sociology of Race and Ethnicity* 4(1): 1–13.

Szkupinski, Seline Quiroga. 2007. "Blood Is Thicker than Water: Policing Donor Insemination and the Reproduction of Whiteness." *Hypatia: A journal of Feminist Philosophy* 22(2): 143–175.

Tate, Shirley Ann. 2007. "Black Beauty: Shade, Hair and Anti-Racist Aesthetics." *Ethnic and Racial Studies* 30(2): 300–319.

Taylor, Mildred D. 1981. *Let the Circle be Unbroken*. London: Dial Press.

Teague, Andy. 2000. "New Methodologies for the 2001 Census in England and Wales." *International Journal of Social Research Methodology* 3(3): 245–255.

Telles, Edward E. 2006. *Race in Another America: The Significance of Skin Color in Brazil.* Princeton, NJ: Princeton University Press.

The Guardian. 2017. "'I Love the Idea of a Mixed-Race Princess': Readers on the Royal Engagement." 27 November. Retrieved 28 November 2017 (https://www.theguardian.com/uk-news/2017/nov/27/readers-on-the-royal-engagement-prince-harry-meghan-markle).

Thompson, Beverly. 2000a. "Multiplicity in Identity Politics' Monoculture: Towards a Multiracial/Bisexual Theory." *Thamyris* 7(1 & 2): 99–122.

Thompson, Beverly. 2000b. "Fence Sitters, Switch Hitters, and Bi-Bi- Girls: An Exploration of 'Hapa' and Bisexual Identities." *Frontiers: A Journal of Women Studies* 21(1/2): 171–180.

Thompson, Beverly. 2012. "The Price of 'Community' from Bisexual/Biracial Women's Perspectives." *Journal of Bisexuality* 12: 417–428.

Thompson, Debra. 2015. "The Ethnic Question: Census Politics in Great Britain." Pp. 111–139 in *Social Statistics and Ethnic Diversity: Cross-National Perspectives in Classifications and Identity Politics*, edited by P. Simon, V. Piché, and A. A. Gagnon. Springer Open.

Townsend, Sarah S. M., Hazel R. Markus, and Hilary B. Bergsieker. 2009. "My Choice, Your Categories: The Denial of Multiracial Identities." *Journal of Social Issues* 65(1): 185–204.

Tuan, Mia. 1998. *Forever Foreigners or Honorary Whites? The Asian Ethnic Experience Today.* New Brunswick, NJ: Rutgers University Press.

United Nations. 2017. *Principles and Recommendations for Population and Housing Censuses.* Revision Three. Department of Economic and Social Affairs Statistic Division. New York, NY: United Nations Publication.

United States Census Bureau. 2019. "Questionnaires." 28 January. Retrieved 12 February 2019 (https://www.census.gov/history/www/through_the_decades/questionnaires).

van Dijk, Teun A. 1993. *Elite Discourse and Racism.* Newbury Park, CA: SAGE Publications.

van Dijk, Teun A. 2001. "Multidisciplinary CDA: A Plea for Diversity." Pp. 95–121 in *Methods of Critical Discourse Analysis*, edited by R. Wodak and M. Meyer. London: SAGE Publications

Vasquez, Jessica M. 2010. "Blurred Borders for Some but Not 'Others': Racialization, 'Flexible Ethnicity,' Gender, and Third-generation Mexican American Identity." *Sociological Perspectives* 53(1): 45–71.

Vasquez-Tokos, Jessica. 2017. "'If I Can Offer You Some Advice': Rapport and Data Collection in Interviews Between Adults of Different Ages." *Symbolic Interaction* 40(4): 466–482.

Vidal-Ortiz, Salvado, Brandon Andrew Robinson, and Cristina Khan. 2018. *Race and Sexuality.* Cambridge: Polity Press.

Wade, Lisa. 2017. *American Hookup: The New Culture of Sex on Campus.* New York, NY: W.W. Norton & Company.

Waring, Chandra D. L. 2013. "'They See Me as Exotic … That Intrigues Them:' Gender, Sexuality and the Racially Ambiguous Body." *Race, Gender & Class* 20(3–4): 299–317.

Washington, Myra S. 2017. *Blasian Invasion: Racial Mixing in the Celebrity Industrial Complex.* Jackson, MS: University Press of Mississippi.

Waters, Mary C. 1990. *Ethnic Options: Choosing Identities in America.* Berkeley, CA: University of California Press.

West, Candice and Don H. Zimmerman. 1987. "Doing Gender." *Gender and Society* 1(2): 125–151.

West, Candice and Sarah Fenstermaker. 1995. "Doing Difference." *Gender and Society* 9(1): 837.

Whisnant, Clayton J. 2009. *Foucault & Discourse: A Handout for HIS389*. Wofford College. Retrieved 15 December 2016 (http://webs.wofford.edu/whisnantcj/his389/foucault_discourse.pdf).

White, Emma. 2012. "Ethnicity and National Identity in England and Wales: 2011." *Ethnicity and National Identity in England and Wales*. London: Office for National Statistics.

White Paper. 1999. *The 2001 Census of Population*. London: Crown: The Stationery Office Limited.

White Paper. 2003. *Ethnic Group Statistics: A Guide for the Collection and Classification of Ethnicity Data*. London: Crown. Published with the permission of the Controller of Her Majesty's Stationary Office.

Williams, Kim M. 2005. "Multiracialism and the Civil Rights Future." *Daedalus* 134(1): 53-60.

Williams, Kim M. 2006. *Mark One or More: Civil rights in the Multiracial Era*. Ann Arbor, MI: University of Michigan Press.

Williams-León, Teresa and Cynthia Nakashima, eds. 2001. *The Sum of Our Parts: Mixed-Heritage Asian Americans*. Philadelphia, PA: Temple University Press.

Winters, Loretta I. and Herman DeBose, eds. 2003. *New Faces in a Changing America: Multiracial Identity in the 21st Century*. Newbury Park, CA: SAGE Publications.

Wise, Timothy. 2010. *Colorblind: The Rise of Post-Racial Politics and the Retreat from Racial Equity*. San Francisco, CA: City Lights Open Publishers.

Zack, Naomi, ed. 1995. *American Mixed Race: The Culture of Microdiversity*. Lanham, MD: Rowman & Littlefield Publishers, Inc.

Zack, Naomi. 2002. *Philosophy of Science and Race*. New York, NY: Routledge.

Index

www.ingramcontent.com/pod-product-compliance
Lightning Source LLC
Chambersburg PA
CBHW050612280326
41932CB00016B/3009